BACK FROM THE BRINK

BACK FROM THE BRINK

NANCY F. CASTALDO

Houghton Mifflin Harcourt
Boston New York

It is said that when courage, genius, and generosity hold hands, all things are possible. This book is dedicated to all those who join hands in making the impossible a reality. You are all my heroes!

hmhco.com

The text type was set in Mercury Text G2.
The display type was set in Veneer.
Photo credits:
13: Judy Bryan for Nancy F. Castaldo; 16: Used by permission of International Crane Foundation; 21: Used by permission of International Crane Foundation; 26: Sara Zimorski, Louisiana Department of Natural Resources; 32: From the deGrummond Children's Book Collection; 58–60: Used by permission of George Steele; 120: Lori Oberhofer/NPS; 131: Library of Congress; 133: Photographer unknown/NPS; 135: Photographer unknown, 1930/NPS; 137: J Schmidt/NPS; All other photos are by Nancy F. Castaldo.

Library of Congress Cataloging-in-Publication Data

Names: Castaldo, Nancy F. (Nancy Fusco), 1962– , author.
Title: Back from the brink / by Nancy F. Castaldo.
Description: Boston : Houghton Mifflin Harcourt, 2018. | Includes bibliographical references. | Audience: Ages 10 to 12. | Audience: Grades4 to 6.
Identifiers: LCCN 2017015664 | ISBN 9780544953437
Subjects: LCSH: Endangered species—United States—Juvenile literature. | Wildlife conservation—United States—Juvenile literature. | Wildlife recovery—United States—Juvenile literature.
Classification: LCC QL84.2 .C37 2018 | DDC 333.95/220973—dc23
LC record available at https://lccn.loc.gov/2017015664

Manufactured in China
SCP 10 9 8 7 6 5 4 3 2 1
4500694562

CONTENTS

"When the last individual of a race of living things breathes no more, another heaven and another earth must pass before such a one can be again."

—William Beebe, 1906

"Nothing is more priceless and more worthy of preservation than the rich array of animal life with which our country has been blessed. It is a many-faceted treasure, of value to scholars, scientists, and nature lovers alike, and it forms a vital part of the heritage we all share as Americans."

—Richard Nixon, upon signing the
Endangered Species Act, 1973

Everglades National Park in Florida is home to several threatened and endangered species including the Florida panther, American alligator, snail kite, and the wood stork.

THE PATH TO PRESERVATION

We are not alone on this great spinning planet. Alongside us are countless creatures with whom we share the earth's space and resources. Sometimes we collide, and when we do, it's usually the animals that lose out.

Those "collisions" seem to be happening more frequently as the human population grows and our planet is taxed. We are seeing an unprecedented loss of creatures across the globe. Many scientists claim that we are undergoing the sixth great era of mass extinction of biodiversity in the course of our planet's life. Although the other eras of mass extinction have occurred as a result of natural causes, this is the first one that plants humans squarely in the realm of responsibility. It isn't an ice age or an asteroid that is causing so many of these creatures to be doomed; it's things such as hunting, habitat destruction, and climate change that are wreaking havoc on our wildlife. Once a mass extinction occurs, it takes millions of years for life on the planet to recover, and when it does, it looks wildly different. It is frightening and heartbreaking to witness this loss of biodiversity, but in its midst are stories of hope. All is not lost.

Each of the species in this book has played a critical role in the environment and each reached the brink of extinction. American alligators were overhunted. Giant tortoises suffered from the introduction of invasive alien species. Eagles were devastated by the use of pesticides. And buffalo were slaughtered mercilessly in an attempt to civilize the American West. All of these animal populations plummeted, and yet, all of them survive today.

Their roads to recovery have been equally unique. From California condors—which were controversially removed from the wild for a chance at a captive breeding program—to humans teaching whooping cranes how to migrate, their stories of survival are equally diverse.

At the heart of each story are both the important legislation that affords protection for these creatures and the dedicated people who couldn't imagine a world without them. Such people as William Hornaday, Aldo Leopold, Rachel Carson, Farley Mowat, and President Richard Nixon recognized the vital role of wildlife in our world, along with countless volunteers, scientists, and conservationists who have followed their example and leadership.

THE ENDANGERED SPECIES ACT

More than forty years ago, on December 28, 1973, President Richard Nixon sat down in San Clemente, California, with pen in hand and signed the Endangered Species Act. This wasn't his first "green" action as president. He had already signed legislation for the National Environmental Policy Act and signed an executive order to create the Environmental Protection Agency (EPA).

Nixon and Congress recognized that the United States was at a crossroads. There was an international list of threatened species known as the Red List, which was compiled by the International Union for Conservation of Nature (IUCN). And Congress had passed the Endangered Species Preservation Act in 1966. But the United States did not have a federal list to protect species that were in trouble. More needed to be done. Bison bones were scattered across the prairie. The population of our national bird was plummeting, owing to rampant pesticide use. We were losing treasured wildlife; we had already lost some, including the passenger pigeon.

President Nixon, understanding that our place in the world, as well as our advantages, could lead to a great crisis, said, "What we really confront here is that in the highly industrialized, richest countries, we have the greatest danger. Because of our wealth we can afford the automobiles, we can afford all the things that pollute the air, pollute the water, and make this really a poisonous world in which to live."

ECO-HERO: PRESIDENT NIXON'S GREEN LEGACY

1969—President Nixon called for a stop to Great Lakes dumping.

1970—President Nixon created a cabinet-level Council on Environmental Quality.

1970–72—The EPA was created and the Clean Water Act was passed.

1972—The Marine Mammal Protection Act was passed.

THE ENDANGERED SPECIES ACT

The ESA states, "The purposes of this Act are to provide a means whereby the ecosystems upon which endangered species and threatened species depend may be conserved, to provide a program for the conservation of such endangered species and threatened species, and to take such steps as may be appropriate to achieve the purposes of the treaties and conventions set forth in subsection (a) of this section. It is further declared to be the policy of Congress that all Federal departments and agencies shall seek to conserve endangered species and threatened species and shall utilize their authorities in furtherance of the purposes of this Act."

ESA VS. SARA VS. THE RED LIST

The United States' Endangered Species Act (ESA) has a counterpart in Canada known as the Species at Risk Act (SARA). Unlike the ESA, evaluations of species listed in SARA are all conducted by a single Canadian scientific office, which can be beneficial. But the ESA has something SARA doesn't. Decisions on listing species under the ESA depend only on species population and cannot legally consider socioeconomic factors, which can be considered under SARA—a plus for United States species. Both of these policy particulars are strengths that, if combined, would benefit all North American endangered species.

The Red List is different from both the ESA and SARA. It is not country specific but lists globally threatened species under an international group of organizations collectively known as the International Union for Conservation of Nature. Its aim is to bring an awareness of these threatened species to the public and to international policymakers. Globally recognized scientists such as the United States' Joe Wasilewski contribute their expertise. Joe is a wildlife biologist who serves on both the IUCN's Crocodile Specialist Group and the Iguana Specialist Group.

It was, as President Nixon said in 1970, "now or never."

In 1972, President Nixon told the nation that existing laws were insufficient to "save a vanishing species." He and Congress recognized that the Endangered Species Act would be able to provide federal protection for threatened species and hopefully reverse their decline.

Congress, along with a team of scientists and lawyers, drafted this important legislation. The Senate unanimously passed the bill and two months later the House passed it with a vote of 390 to 12. It was signed into law on December 12, 1973. It put our native wildlife species in a position of importance and authorized agencies to act on their behalf.

RECOVERY

When a species is placed on the federal List of Endangered and Threatened Wildlife or the List of Endangered or Threatened Plants, the United States government is obligated to make plans for the recovery of that species, protect critical habitat, and restrict the trade or hunting of that species. At present, there are about six hundred recovery plans in the works to rescue listed species in this country. That's pretty comforting, isn't it? And the Endangered Species Act has not only saved many species, it has created thousands of jobs.

At a time when our population keeps growing and we face changes in our global climate, isn't it a relief to know that there are measures in place

The Los Angeles Zoo's condor recovery team works side by side with the U.S. Fish and Wildlife Service to keep records and manage the California condor population.

that can look out for the needs of the creatures that cohabit this planet, even when these needs may conflict with our short-term economic goals?

Scientists around the world have been instrumental in the recovery plans that have been developed for our most critical species, from sea turtles to pandas, and we rely on international governments to help develop these plans. Scientists often come up with drastic solutions in the hope that they can reverse, or at least stop, further loss of a population.

WORKING TOGETHER

As long as we share the planet with wild creatures, there will be some that will suffer from habitat loss, overhunting, climate change, and other issues that will have an impact on their population, but we do have the ability to make a difference in many of their stories. As the stories ahead prove, we can work together to repair the damage before it is too late.

Cans of turtle soup could once be found in grocery stores alongside cans of tomato soup. Thanks to federal protections, eating turtle soup is a crime today in the U.S.

WHOOPING CRANES IN THE WETLANDS

THE LAND OF COWS AND CRANES

It's autumn, and the Wisconsin cornfields have been harvested, the trees are turning brilliant shades of red and orange. I've come to this part of North America to see something very special—endangered whooping cranes (*Grus americana*). There are only a few places in North America where these birds can be seen, and I'm at one of them—the International Crane Foundation (ICF) in Baraboo, Wisconsin.

I follow a winding path to the whooping crane exhibit. Along the way, I see other crane species from all over the world, including the fancy crowned cranes from Africa and the graceful gray sandhill cranes that the conservationist Aldo Leopold described nearby in his famous journal.

The whooping crane exhibit is at the end of the path, through a pavilion. I open a door leading to the crane's wetland habitat outside . . . and there they are, standing among the tall green reeds, two striking white cranes with brilliant red-capped heads.

Whooping cranes are omnivores, meaning they eat plants and animals, including insects, fish, and frogs.

ECO-HERO ALDO LEOPOLD

The author, scientist, conservationist, and philosopher Aldo Leopold is known by many as the father of wildlife ecology. He developed the idea for a "land ethic," which called for a caring and thoughtful relationship between humans and wild America. Much of his conservation writing was inspired by the detailed journals he wrote in his famous woodland shack beside the Wisconsin River, where he lived with his family.

Aldo Leopold's shack still stands to inspire visitors today.

First spotted by the explorer Philip Amadas in 1589 off the coast of North Carolina, this majestic species once lived everywhere from the Arctic coast to central Mexico, from Utah east to New Jersey, and into South Carolina, Georgia, and Florida. They even flew into the Canadian provinces of Manitoba, Saskatchewan, and Alberta. But by 1941, that was not the case. The population of whooping cranes had dwindled to a flock of just sixteen birds that migrated twenty-five hundred miles each year between Canada, where they spent the summer, and the southern state of Texas, where they remained for the winter. There was also a small flock of six nonmigratory birds that lived full-time in Louisiana. Unfortunately, by 1950, the Louisiana birds had perished, leaving only the sixteen migratory birds left in the wild.

Only sixteen birds. Imagine that!

How in the world did their population plummet to such a tiny number?

HUNTED TO THE BRINK

I watch as two cranes duck out from behind the reeds, dipping their beaks in and out of the water, searching for grasses as well as snails and other wetland creatures. Whooping cranes are huge birds. I can imagine how dramatic their white feathers must have looked in women's hats in the late 1800s.

The size and the striking white feathers of these cranes made them easy targets for hunters and specimen collectors. Unfortunately, their decreasing numbers only encouraged collectors to gather the rare eggs and birds for their specimen collections.

But that wasn't all. As with most endangered species, multiple factors caused the population to drop. In this case, when people turned nesting wetlands into farmland, humans did further damage by moving into the cranes' habitat. This left the birds without a place to live or raise their young.

FEATHERS FOR HATS

Whooping cranes were not the only birds being hunted for their plumage. Some fifty North American species were slaughtered for their feathers in the late nineteenth century. "It was a common thing for a rookery of several hundred birds to be attacked by the plume hunters, and in two or three days utterly destroyed," wrote William Hornaday, director of the New York Zoological Society and formerly chief taxidermist at the Smithsonian.

It took two women in Boston to lead a revolt against this practice. Hurrah for cousins Minna Hall and Harriet Hemenway, whose efforts led to the passage of the Migratory Bird Treaty Act (1918), which protects birds, their nests, and their eggs.

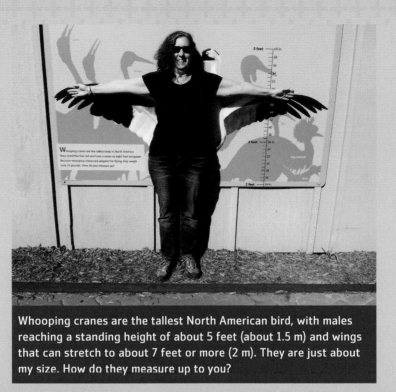

Whooping cranes are the tallest North American bird, with males reaching a standing height of about 5 feet (about 1.5 m) and wings that can stretch to about 7 feet or more (2 m). They are just about my size. How do they measure up to you?

Eventually the entire population was contained within one flock of sixteen. And although scientists knew where in Texas the birds spent the winter—an area that later became the Aransas National Wildlife Refuge—they did not know specifically where their breeding grounds were—only that they were in northern Canada. Had they known, they might have been able to develop a plan for the cranes' recovery.

The National Audubon Society mounted an investigation into the biology and population of whooping cranes in the 1940s, joining with the U.S. Fish and Wildlife Service to form the Cooperative Whooping Crane

Project in 1945. Robert P. Allen, often frustrated by fruitless air searches, spent years following the cranes' migration route. The expeditions were dangerous and unsuccessful.

By chance, a fire crew flying over the northern edge of Canada's Wood Buffalo National Park in 1954 spotted where the birds were laying their eggs and raising their chicks. It was just the break the scientists needed! These whooping cranes were found to lay two eggs in each clutch, but each pair was successfully raising only one chick. Scientists thought that maybe they could remove that extra egg from each clutch and incubate it with foster sandhill crane parents or in an incubator.

From 1967 to 1996, conservationists collected eggs from that wild flock. It wasn't easy to transport these eggs in the early days of the recovery program. In 1975, whooping crane eggs were flown twelve hundred miles, from Canada to a refuge in Idaho, in a special insulated suitcase. The shallow meadow wetland in Idaho was a historically successful sandhill crane nesting site. Each whooping crane egg was placed in a sandhill crane nest. Conservationists worked fast to move these eggs: nest-to-nest transfer took just thirty-two hours.

"Sympathy for the species is widespread and there seems no reason to doubt that many others would be glad to assist in the efforts towards its survival. The whooping crane, in its fight for existence, has an appeal for all of us. What could be more fitting than that many hands be raised to save it." —field biologist Robert P. Allen, 1952

The ICF's crane puppets are made to look just like adult whoopers. Their colors and markings help chicks that are cared for by humans recognize their species in the wild and help prevent them from imprinting on their caretakers.

The eggs, incubated by their surrogate sandhill crane parents, and the resulting chicks became the lifeblood of the recovery program.

GEORGE, TEX, AND GEE WHIZ!

The San Antonio Zoo in Texas was one of the places where people were desperately trying to breed whooping cranes. Although more than fifty eggs were hatched there (from the only whooping crane pair in captivity), only one chick survived. The hand-reared chick was named Tex.

Tex had a hard time figuring out whether she was a bird or a human. Instead of imprinting on her crane parents, the way baby birds do in the wild, she imprinted on the humans raising her.

Brought to International Crane Foundation (ICF) in 1976, she developed a special relationship with the ornithologist George Archibald, cofounder of the ICF. George was determined to have Tex help the whooping crane population survive.

George and Tex spent many hours together. The two would walk around the foundation each morning, George dancing like a whooping crane, trying to teach Tex how to be a crane and respond to crane courtship. The team working with George provided male whooping crane sperm to fertilize Tex's eggs, but when Tex finally did lay an egg, it was found to be unfertilized. The next year, Tex laid a fertile egg. Everyone was excited, especially George, but sadly, the little chick died just before hatching. Biologists tried again in 1979, but the egg Tex laid that year had a very soft shell, too soft for a chick to survive. Perhaps Tex would never be able to help bring more whooping cranes into the population. But the team didn't give up.

ICF cofounder George Archibald taking his daily walk with Tex.

Finally, success. On June 3, 1982, one of Tex's eggs hatched. The baby male chick was named Gee Whiz.

So much was riding on this tiny chick. If Gee Whiz flourished, it meant that biologists could breed others and grow the population. If he didn't, it could mean that the species had a good chance of becoming extinct.

But the little chick was tiny and underweight. It didn't look good. In a last-ditch effort to keep the baby alive, George placed the tiniest tube in his beak and slowly fed him drops of water.

Gee Whiz survived!

That important little chick recently celebrated his thirty-fifth birthday. He has been the father of many whooping cranes, too—in fact, as of 2016, he had 20 crane kids, 97 grand-cranes, and 22 great-grand-cranes. That's a whopping 139 whoopers for the crane population.

HAND-RAISING BIRDS

Raising a baby bird is very labor-intensive and can be hard on the baby bird, especially if it is wild. Young whooping cranes have to be fed every fifteen to twenty minutes from sunrise to sunset, often by a human wearing a whooping crane costume or using a crane hand puppet to discourage the chick from imprinting on humans. As a bird matures in the wild, adult birds teach it the skills it needs to survive. Hand-reared birds miss out on acquiring those skills. Tex was one of those birds that missed out on learning her "bird" skills.

IN THE WILD

It is because of the ICF's dedication and the cooperation of other organizations that we still have any whooping cranes in the wild. Conservationists and government agencies worked diligently to protect the flock and encourage the birds to breed. The birds were listed as endangered in the United States in 1966 and in Canada in 1978. By 1970, recovery efforts had successfully grown the small flock to fifty-seven birds. By 2005 it had reached more than two hundred.

The recovery plan was enlarged in 1995 when the two teams were combined into the International Whooping Crane Recovery Team, which is made up of five Canadians appointed by the Canadian Wildlife Service and five Americans appointed by the U.S. Fish and Wildlife Service. The new team worked to introduce cranes to Florida, but those birds never learned to migrate naturally. To solve this problem, the team set out to teach the birds how to migrate between Wisconsin and Florida. They had to accomplish this without the help of adult birds, implementing a risky plan to use an ultralight aircraft to demonstrate the migration flight to the young whooping cranes.

FLIGHT TO FLORIDA

On September 20, 2015, a flock of six young whooping cranes was scheduled to take off for their fall migration from Wisconsin to Florida. But their departure was delayed. Unharvested crops still filled the fields where the cranes would land, so the team needed to wait a bit, until the southern harvest was finished for the season and the birds could land safely. The weather wasn't cooperating. Fog and wind hampered the ultralight that guided them to their winter roost.

This was not the first flight for the whooper-guiding ultralight. The first aircraft-guided whooping crane migration occurred in 2001, and every year after that until 2015.

When baby whoopers are hatched in captivity, they are given two leg bands—one that allows scientists to track them through a radio transmitter, the other a U.S. Fish and Wildlife Service metal identification band. If the chicks had been born in the wild, their parents would have taught them how to migrate, but these young ones needed a little help. The ultralight flown by a human was their surrogate teacher. It flew to Florida each year, with the young birds following behind. The birds and the ultralight would fly and make stops along the journey to rest and eat. Once in Florida, the birds would join the flock and from then on would know the migration route.

Eventually, after 115 days of flying and resting, the 2015 journey was complete.

But after reviewing the data on the reintroduced flock, scientists have recently discovered some troubling news. The flock, once it reached Florida each year, was not having success at raising its own chicks. Only one chick survived out of twenty-three hatched in the summer of 2016. The entire breeding program was examined. Maybe the cranes needed to be reared by other cranes to learn how to parent—and not by the costumed human surrogate parents.

A NEW PLAN

A new plan was devised in which captive-hatched chicks would be raised by a pair of cranes within a captive breeding flock.

There was already another successful migration program in place, called Direct Autumn Release (DAR), in which chicks were released near adult whooping cranes in the hopes that the adults would lead them on the migration path after their flight feathers developed and they were ready to fledge. Scientists believed that, as with the ultralight migration, once the birds learned the migration route, they would use it for the rest of their lives.

Starting in 2016, the fledglings were released only with experienced adult cranes to guide them. With the new crane–crane rearing method, letting the adult cranes guide the chicks on their migration journey, biologists hoped the cranes would be more successful in rearing their own young.

Scientists tracked the first three chicks. The first, number 69-16, was released in Wisconsin near one of the previous year's crane-reared cranes. In October she flew off with some sandhill cranes and stopped in Indiana for several days. She then continued on to Alabama. She is still being monitored.

Young whoopers sport a mottled coat of brown and white feathers to help keep them camouflaged in the wild.

The second, 71-16, nicknamed Smoky, was released in Wisconsin in September and flew to another area in Wisconsin in October. He is still being monitored. The third, 70-16, nicknamed Bryce, was released in November but missed the window for flying south before the poor weather set in. Bryce ended up needing to catch a ride to Florida with ICF staff .

CRANE FUTURE

No one imagined there would ever be enough whooping cranes to reintroduce the species to the eastern United States, but there are more than 600 whooping cranes in the world today. More than half are members of the Aransas–Wood Buffalo historic migratory flock. Reintroduced populations make up the second highest number, with close to 100 forming the eastern migratory flock, nearly 40 living full-time in Louisiana, and another 10 or

What you can do: Report whooping crane sightings at: www.fws.gov/midwest/whoopingcrane/sightings/sightingform.cfm.

CRANES AND CONDORS

In 2001 a whooping crane report cited similarities between whooping crane recovery and California condor recovery, demonstrating how important it is for scientists to compare the successes and failures of their distinct recovery plans. It's always beneficial to keep communications open and scientific studies available so that all species benefit.

so living full-time in Florida. The rest, about 160, are in captivity, helping scientists learn more about cranes and growing their population.

People, too, flock to see the birds in Texas—approximately eighty thousand people each year, usually from mid-November through March, when the cranes are enjoying their winter grounds. The whoopers attract roughly $6 million in revenue from travel to the area each year.

Conservationists are working toward the long-term recovery goal of a healthy population of at least a thousand whoopers in North America by 2035. That does seem a long way away, but when a species population has decreased to the brink of extinction, it might take many, many years for it to recover, if it does at all. Scientists must often think far into the future. There is no quick fix.

CRANE CRIME

It would be wonderful if whooping cranes were never hunted again, yet even though it is now a crime to kill an endangered whooping crane, there are still people who do. In October 2016, nineteen-year-old Joseph Frederick was given a stiff sentence for shooting and killing two whooping cranes in Texas. The judge made him pay more than $25,000 and sentenced him to two hundred hours of community service with Texas Parks and Wildlife or the U.S. Fish and Wildlife Service (USFWS).

In January 2017 one of the migrating female breeding whoopers en route from Wisconsin to Florida was shot by a poacher in Indiana. A reward was posted for information leading to an arrest.

But challenges still exist for the wild population. Whooping cranes take between three and five years to reach maturity. They mate for life, and pairs often only raise one offspring. The loss of that one bird, caused by a natural or unnatural death, can be a devastating blow to the entire population.

WHOOPERS NEED WETLANDS

Whooping cranes, unlike their close cousins the sandhill cranes, need wetland habitat to raise their young. They also require wetlands for stops during migration. The preservation of wetland habitat is still crucial.

Other factors that make an impact on the crane population are oil spills, human population growth, and hurricanes, which still disrupt breeding and nesting. Illegal hunting and collisions with power lines also contribute to the loss of migrating cranes.

But that's where the combined forces of conservationists, politicians, and volunteers make a difference. They are working hard to ensure that fresh water flows into the coastal bays of Texas—where the cranes live during the winter; that private land is protected so that the cranes have habitat even with rising sea levels on the coast; and that successful breeding programs

PIT STOP

Shallow, temporary wetland ponds provide whoopers with the perfect resting and feeding habitats during their migration. Historically, American bison and wildfires kept the wetlands free from much vegetation. But now that wildfires are controlled and bison do not roam free as they once did, wetland habitats in the whoopers' migration path are crucial.

WHOOPING CRANE 16-11 AND WHOOPSIE

Sometimes a member of a certain species will mate with a member of a related species if a mate of their own species is not available or if they are in a new region. This is something to be more aware of as wildlife populations shift to survive climate change. Like the hybrid grolar bears being born to polar bear and grizzly bear parents, a male whooping crane, number 16-11, nicknamed Grasshopper, found his mate within a sandhill crane flock.

As a chick, 16-11 was raised by humans in crane costumes and then released. The expectation was that he would learn how to be a whooping crane from the resident sandhill cranes, but when he came of age, he didn't have any female whoopers to mate with in the refuge. Instead, he found his mate among the sandhill cranes, and their hybrid chick was born in Wisconsin's Horicon National Wildlife Refuge, the first wild whooper born there. It was being raised by 16-11 when conservationists from the International Crane Foundation stepped in. The tiny, fluffy chick was a hybrid, having traits from both species. Known as a whoophill crane, he received the nickname Whoopsie.

The young hybrid crane would hamper the recovery of endangered whooping cranes in the wild because it would not be able to breed and grow the flock with more whooping cranes. Whoopsie was captured in 2015 and paired with a female sandhill crane at the ICF to help incubate whooping crane eggs. His whooping crane dad, 16-11, was also brought into captivity—to a Florida breeding center for endangered species—in the hopes that the strong parenting skills he had demonstrated with the sandhill crane would make him a valuable member of a captive whooping crane flock.

continue to increase the crane population. Outreach to make hunters and residents allies in the protection of wetlands is ongoing. Many people in Alabama, for example, didn't even know that there were whooping cranes wintering in their state. We can all help to get the word out about cranes! Join in the Give a Whoop campaign and be a crane advocate in your area. Protecting wetlands helps not only cranes, but lots of other wildlife.

HAPPY BIRTH DAY!

Every birthday is special, but this whooping crane's birthday is worthy of a major celebration. Louisiana hadn't seen any baby whoopers in more than seventy-five years! After losing the state's resident non-migratory flock so many decades ago, conservationists and government agencies struggled to preserve wetlands and encourage reintroduced whooping cranes to breed. The 2016 birth—the first wild birth since the repopulation program began five years before—marked a milestone.

Good news! In 2016, the first wild whooper was hatched in Louisiana since World War II.

"This is something we've been looking forward to and anticipating since the reintroduction began in 2011," said biologist Sara Zimorski of the Louisiana Department of Wildlife and Fisheries, who leads the Louisiana Whooping Crane Project. "One of the major steps in restoring the species is successful reproduction. We've had several pairs nesting the last couple of years, but until now no favorable outcomes. It's an exciting time for us and all of our partners who have worked so hard alongside us."

Like its relatives who lived year-round in Louisiana so long ago, this young bird will be part of a resident flock.

"This couldn't have been done without the assistance of private landowners. The support and cooperation of the many landowners and farmers on whose property the birds spend time is critical to the success of the project," says Zimorski.

SANDBARS AND SANDHILL CRANES

After my time with the cranes at the International Crane Foundation, I stop at Aldo Leopold's historic shack. I walk beside the Wisconsin River behind it in the hopes of seeing sandhill cranes in the wild. These crane cousins can still be seen in large flocks, but this afternoon the sandbars are quiet.

It isn't until I am driving to the airport the next day that I see a group of sandhill cranes standing in a cornfield. I want to stop to admire their grace and beauty, but my flight won't wait.

Let's hope that one day whooping cranes might be as common a sight as their cousins.

Not all gray wolves are gray in color. Their fur can range from white-gray to brown or black to cream or even tan; gray is, however, a dominant color.

WOLVES IN THE WILD

A WOLF HOWLS

The walk up the long drive to the Wolf Conservation Center (WCC) in South Salem, New York, is quiet except for a cool spring wind rustling the budded tree branches. Even the jet-black crows sitting atop the fences and the turkey vultures circling overhead don't break the quiet of the serene afternoon. But as we reach the path leading to the wolf enclosures, Regan Downey, our guide for the afternoon, stops.

"Before we go any farther, we have to let them know we're coming," she says. "Feel free to join in." With that, she throws her head back and begins to howl. I'm too surprised to join her. She ends in one long note. I'm amazed at how long she can hold it. She finishes, and for just a second there is silence; then the air is filled with countless wolf howls, answering from up ahead. These are the real deal, and they sound unlike anything I have heard in the wild before. I shudder, excited, as the wildness envelops me. It's hard to believe that I am not even an hour and a half away from the honking horns of New York City.

We continue to walk, my pace increasing, until the first of the answering wolves comes into view. These are not wild, free-roaming wolves.

There hasn't been a population of wild, free wolves in New York State since around 1900. The wolves in front of me are residents of the Wolf Conservation Center.

Wolves howl to assemble a pack, warn other creatures to stay away, or to initiate a hunt.

AMBASSADOR WOLVES

I approach the enclosure housing the ambassador gray wolf (*Canis lupus occidentalis*) pack that serves to educate the public about the species. Alawa, pronounced *ai-lay-ewa,* is Algonquin for "Sweet Pea." She has a beautiful light brown and gray, almost white, coat. She looks more like some sort of spirit animal than the dog cousin she is. She shares the enclosure with her brothers, Nikai—meaning "Little Saint" or "One Who Wanders"—and striking, coal-black Zephyr, meaning "light or west wind."

As I focus my camera lens on Nikai's mesmerizing orange wolf eyes, the words of Minnesota congressman Robert Bergland enter my mind. I remember reading them in the discussion regarding the passing of the Endangered Species Act in December 1973. "The wolf is a problem," he said emphatically.

Gazing at the lounging wolf in front of me, it's Henry David Thoreau's words I choose to ponder instead: "Life consists with wildness. The most alive is the wildest. Not yet subdued to man, its presence refreshes him."

Zephyr, one of the Wolf Conservation Center's ambassador wolves, is a mix of gray wolf subspecies but is primarily Canadian/ Rocky Mountain gray wolf (*Canis lupus occidentalis*).

THE BIG BAD WOLF

Wolves have been demonized for centuries. You'll know this firsthand if you are a fairy-tale reader! Just think of the menacing Big Bad Wolf in "Little Red Riding Hood" and the "Three Little Pigs," or of mythic, shapeshifting werewolves!

As carnivores high on the food chain, wolves have been unwelcome to ranchers and townspeople alike. In fact, as early as 1638, when fear ran rampant in colonial America, a law in Massachusetts encouraged wolves to be shot on sight within a town.

Montana enacted its first bounty on wolves in 1884. Several years later, in 1909, readers of the Eugene *Register-Guard* opened their newspapers to find that the state of Oregon had also put out a bounty on coyotes and wolves. The bounty would bring hunters $5.00 for each gray (*Canis lupus*) or black wolf (not a separate species but a color variant of *Canis lupus*) and $2.50 for each wolf pup. This was at a time when 14 cents could buy a dozen eggs and a quart of milk cost only 8 cents. Think of how valuable $5.00 was at that time.

Through 1918, bounties were paid for more than eighty thousand wolves. In 1947, for a $25 bounty, Oregon's last wolf was killed. It's no wonder that the population of any wolf species dwindled close to the point of no return.

W. W. Denslow's illustrations for the historic 1903 version of *Little Red Riding Hood*.

"Good morning, Red Riding Hood," said the gaunt gray wolf, as he stood in her path, and sniffed at her basket, "what have you there?"

"Some cheese cakes and sweets, for granny dear," said she, "so get out of my way, and let me go on, for I must hurry." She did not like the hungry look of the wolf, nor the gleam of his cruel looking teeth, when he smiled and tried to look pleasant.

It made the hungry wolf's mouth water, when he heard of all those good things, and as he was a greedy robber, he had a great mind to take them away from Riding Hood, and eat them up. But when he heard the ring of the woodman's ax, as he chopped at the sturdy oaks, near by, he was afraid that a call from Riding Hood would get him into trouble, so, as he was a crafty old wolf, he simply said, with a smile,

Ambassador wolves prove that wolves are not big and bad by inspiring children and adults to understand the importance of wolves in the wild environment.

These canine eyes looking back at me have an uncanny familiarity, but they are wild. They are not like those of my dog. They belong to a part of us that yearns for the mountain path that takes us out of our ordinary lives and into the unknown, the wild part of nature.

Aldo Leopold spoke of those eyes during one of his hunting expeditions. "We reached the old wolf in time to watch a fierce green fire dying in her eyes. I realized then, and have known ever since, that there was something new to me in those eyes—something known only to her and to the mountain. I was young then, and full of trigger-itch; I thought that because fewer wolves meant more deer, that no wolves would mean hunters' paradise. But after seeing the green fire die, I sensed that neither the wolf nor the mountain agreed with such a view," Leopold wrote in *A Sand County Almanac* in 1949.

Aldo Leopold's mountain was right. Fewer wolves do not create a hunter's paradise.

WOLVES AND THE ENVIRONMENT

With any of these species, the question is always raised—why? Why allow a species to exist? Why allow it to recover? And why does it deserve our protection?

Wolves, like any species brought back from the brink, play an important role in our environment. Reintroducing wolves into Yellowstone National Park has demonstrated the importance of the relationship that an apex individual—the top predator in an ecosystem—has with its environment and the cascade that follows. Prior to the wolf reintroduction, Yellowstone suffered owing to a large population of deer that grazed on all the vegetation. Once the wolves were brought back, the deer altered their behavior. They stopped grazing in the gorges and valleys that left them open to predation. Trees began to return and grow into forests. Songbird populations grew. Scientists also found that the wolves kept other grazers from eating all the park's berries, which were a food source for many other forms of wildlife.

Then the rivers changed. Beavers returned and built dams. More pools developed, welcoming greater numbers of animal and fish species. The forests stabilized the riverbanks, and the vegetation growing along them prevented erosion. The reintroduction of the wolves had created a trophic cascade, with all creatures benefiting, as well as the landscape. The wolves had actually changed the geography of the park.

WOLVES IN YELLOWSTONE

After decades of hunting, the last wolf pack in Yellowstone was killed in 1926. In 1973 the gray wolf was listed under the Endangered Species Act as endangered in the United States. A recovery plan was mandated. Even though a process was begun in 1975 to restore wolves to Yellowstone, Congress didn't appropriate money for the plan until 1991. In 1995 and 1996, thirty-one gray wolves from Canada were brought to live in Yellowstone National Park. Ten more were brought to the park in 1997.

BLOODTHIRSTY PREDATORS?

The naturalist and author Farley Mowat wrote of the wolf's plight in his 1963 best-selling book *Never Cry Wolf*. He had been charged with studying the Arctic wolves for the Canadian Wildlife Service. Tales of bloodthirsty wolves slaughtering Arctic caribou brought about the study, but it had a very different outcome from what was expected. Instead of finding the marauding killers he anticipated, Mowat found skillful, protective parents and their young.

In 1973 he added a preface to the book in order to highlight his intentions and the experience he shared with his readers, writing, "Eventually

DEER, WOLVES, AND THE MOUNTAIN

Aldo Leopold wrote again, in "Thinking Like a Mountain," about the complex relationship between wolves, humans, and their mountain environments.

"I now suspect that just as a deer herd lives in mortal fear of its wolves, so does a mountain live in mortal fear of its deer. And perhaps with better cause, for while a buck pulled down by wolves can be replaced in two or three years, a range pulled down by too many deer may fail of replacement in as many decades. So also with cows. The cowman who cleans his range of wolves does not realize that he is taking over the wolf's job of trimming the herd to fit the range. He has not learned to think like a mountain. Hence we have dust bowls, and rivers washing the future into the sea."

Think like a mountain—good advice!

the wolf took the book right out of my hands so that it became a plea for understanding, and preservation, of an extraordinary highly evolved and attractive animal which was, and is, being harried into extinction by the murderous enmity and proclivities of man."

When Mowat added his preface, several species of North American wolf were already virtually extinct. "In the whole of the continental United States (excluding Alaska) probably no more than 1,200 wolves survive," he wrote.

Wolves are responsible for less than 1 percent of lost livestock, but tell that to western ranchers who are on the receiving end of those losses. It was also, and still is, a common belief that wolves kill game that belongs to human hunters. Mowat found that the wolf was actually keeping the caribou healthy by killing inferior animals. This behavior kept the caribou herds—and the environment—strong.

Wolves do not kill for sport. They will, however, sometimes kill more than they can eat at that moment. When a wolf is taking down a caribou cow, the weight difference is staggering. An average wolf might weigh one

A WINTER HUNT BENEFITS ALL

In a hard winter, wolves might be able to take down a few of the weakest and most vulnerable caribou at a time. They will take advantage of that opportunity, but they cannot eat them all at once. They have their fill and return to compete with coyotes, eagles, vultures, and other scavengers for the rest of the carcasses. Their kill supports a host of other species while keeping the herd free of illness.

hundred pounds (45 kg) while a caribou cow can top five hundred pounds (227 kg). According to the Alberta Wilderness Association, wolves actually don't have much success against such large, healthy prey. In fact, when they are hunting moose they kill roughly one in every twelve they have pursued.

A COMMODITY

Wolves have been a commodity, raw material to be bought and sold, but as Maggie Howell, the executive director of the Wolf Conservation Center, reminds me in her office, natural resources belong to everybody.

"The original conservationists have been the hunters. There are consumptive users—hunters—and the nonconsumptive users, the photographers, hikers, and the like. A lot of conservation programs were founded by hunters through licenses and such," she says.

She sits at her desk, the back of her chair featuring a bumper sticker that reads SHOOT COWS NOT WOLVES, and a striking wolf poster hangs above her on the wall. According to Maggie, people who hunt pay a fee for their licenses, but the hikers and people who enjoy just looking at wildlife don't have the same vehicle for funding conservation and therefore have not been as effective as the hunting population and other stakeholders in dictating wildlife management.

"One of the big paradigms [patterns] that we'd like to change is wildlife management and funding," says Maggie.

The Wolf Conservation Center, founded in 1999, teaches the public about wolves, their role in the environment, and how we can protect them.

Conservation efforts are often focused on managing wildlife in the interest of game populations. For example, wolves are looked upon as competing with hunters for the same deer or caribou. If our efforts are focused on maintaining the caribou and deer herds and not considering wolf populations, perhaps our strategy needs to change.

As an example of this, Maggie and I discuss the controversial 2016 killing of gray wolves in British Columbia, which angered conservationists and even drew the attention of the pop singer Miley Cyrus. Shooting wolves from helicopters to control the wolf population is an attempt to keep caribou game herd numbers strong. Cyrus called the wolf cull a "war on wildlife." Maggie's hope is that our focus can shift.

PROTECTED AND HUNTED

Protected against hunting and trapping under the Endangered Species Act one minute and then delisted and hunted the next, wolves have barely survived their violent past. The Endangered Species Act requires the Fish and Wildlife Service to make all decisions based on scientific evidence. When the service is determining whether to list or delist a species, federal law requires that an independent panel of scientists review the facts.

This is not the case with wolves. They are often delisted under pressure by outside interests, and hunting tags are often sold. This has been their unfortunate history. Even the United States government has contributed to these deaths. According to the U.S. Department of Agriculture's (USDA) Animal and Plant Health Inspection Service, between 2004 and 2013 the USDA Wildlife Services program legally killed 3,576 gray wolves and 14 Mexican wolves in order to protect livestock owned by private ranchers. Since the gray wolf was removed from the Endangered Species List under the ESA in 2011, Predator Defense, an organization working to protect and conserve wild predators such as wolves and coyotes, reports that more than 4,200 wolves have been killed in five states.

Just examine the chronology. In 2008, wolves were delisted in Montana, Idaho, and Wyoming. That same year, wolves were back on the list. They were delisted again the following year in Montana and Idaho, but not Wyoming. Four years later wolves were delisted in Wyoming and were classified as predators, able legally to be shot on sight.

Although wolves were reinstated to the federal Endangered Species List by U.S. district judge Beryl Howell following a 2014 lawsuit, they are still being hunted.

It seems that they will continue to be on and off of the Endangered Species List, protected in one state but hunted across the border.

President Nixon wrote to Congress on February 8, 1972, and his words still ring true: "Americans today set high value on the preservation of wildlife. The old notion that 'the only good predator is a dead one' is no longer acceptable as we understand that even the animals and birds which sometimes prey on domesticated animals have their own value in maintaining the balance of nature."

THE WOLVES OF WASHINGTON STATE

There were only ninety gray wolves living in the state of Washington in 2016, and yet eleven of them were targeted for extermination by wildlife officials after reports that calves that had grazed on publicly owned lands had been found dead. The decision came to kill the Profanity Peak pack of six adults and five cubs.

Donny Martorello, director of the Washington Fish and Wildlife Department's wolf policy, said, "The department is committed to wolf recovery, but we also have a shared responsibility to protect livestock from repeated degradation by wolves."

The Center for Biological Diversity (CBD) argues that these wolves are repeatedly being placed in harm's way by the practice of allowing private livestock to graze on thickly forested public lands. Many conservationists believe that those wild areas of our national forests should be places where wolves can roam free without continued efforts to decimate their population.

The ranchers in Washington State whose livestock is killed by endangered wolves are eligible for taxpayer-funded compensation for their losses. So when a wolf preys on their livestock on public national forest land, ranchers not only call for those wolves to be exterminated, they also receive compensation for their losses.

MEXICAN GRAY WOLVES HOWL IN THE WILD AGAIN!

Eleven captive-reared Mexican gray wolves were released into the wilds of Arizona and New Mexico on March 29, 1998. For the first time in more than thirty years, their howl was heard in the Southwest. Celebrate LoboWeek each year on the anniversary of this historic event.

WOLVES IN THE WILD

Gray wolves currently inhabit about 10 percent of their historic range in the continental United States. They can be found only in the Pacific Northwest, near the western Great Lakes, in the northern Rockies, and in southwestern states such as Texas and Louisiana. As many as 11,200 more live in Alaska.

The Canadian/Rocky Mountain gray wolf traditionally roamed in parts of the western continental United States, Alaska, and western Canada.

RED WOLVES STILL ON THE BRINK

Farther up the path at the Wolf Conservation Center is an enclosure housing a pair of red wolves. I stand next to the chainlink fence and peer into the brush on the other side, past the bony remnants of a former meal.

The red wolves are fed a roadkill deer carcass once a week, similar to what they would eat in the wild. The ambassador wolves eat a more eclectic menu of meat donated from farms and Whole Foods supermarkets.

There are ten red wolves at the center. These two are the only ones on view to visitors. Unlike the ambassador pack, they do not come close to the fence to investigate. They remain in the distance, and visitors might see fleeting flashes of red fur moving through the brush.

The red wolves have a different history from that of their gray cousins. They are a species still on the brink. There are only about forty-five to sixty of them living in the wild. Red wolves, listed as endangered in 1967, received a recovery plan in 1973. By 1977 the first litter of pups was born in the breeding program. When they were old enough, those pups were released, making the red wolf the first predatory mammal to be reintroduced to the wild.

These wolves once numbered a mere seventeen in the wild, owing to hunting, trapping, habitat destruction, and poisoning by livestock owners and people who fear them. The species has also faced serious threats from hybridization with coyotes. In 1980 the U.S. Fish and Wildlife Service (USFWS) declared red wolves extinct in the wild. That meant that the only red wolves alive were in captivity.

Thanks to captive breeding programs, the numbers of red wolves, such as the ones at the Wolf Conservation Center, have increased. By 1987, there were enough wolves bred in captivity to begin a reintroduction program. The Wolf Conservation Center has welcomed two litters since 2010. They have also seen one of those wolves take his place in the wilds of North Carolina.

The Wolf Conservation Center was accepted into the Red Wolf Species Survival Plan in 2004. At that time there were only 300 red wolves surviving in the world. Ten now live at the WCC.

Unfortunately, not all has gone well with the USFWS handling of the recovery efforts. There are people who still want wolves removed from the wild and continue to pressure their representatives to petition to have them removed from protection. In 2016, the Center for Biological Diversity, a nonprofit organization focused on preserving biodiversity, filed a lawsuit against the Fish and Wildlife Service for bowing to political pressure to discontinue the recovery program and attempt to delist the wolves. The CBD argues that the agency is letting this species of wolf—which is unique to the United States—go extinct. "It is important because it is a part of our American heritage," said Arkansas State University environmental biology professor Tom Risch about red wolf conservation. "It is the only carnivore that is uniquely ours, and it went extinct in the wild. So we've heard how we need to save the tigers and elephants in the world. Here is a chance we can save an animal in our own backyard."

THE CUSTER WOLF

In 1920 a group of ranchers and other townspeople gathered in Custer, South Dakota. Harry Percival Williams was there to pose for photographs with his prize, the famous Custer wolf, which was renowned as a stealthy assassin of local livestock. But what lay at Williams's feet was an ordinary wolf, barely six feet long, with an aged white pelt. The wolf had a $500 bounty on its head, pretty appealing when the average ranch hand's salary was $25 per week. Williams had been instructed by his supervisor at the U.S. Biological Survey to stay in South Dakota until he killed this wolf. According to the January 17, 1921, press release sent out by the U.S. Department of Agriculture, this wolf was the "master criminal of the animal world." For nine years the wolf had escaped traps, poison, and hunters.

THE WOLF CONSERVATION CENTER'S PACK!

The WCC's PACK Fellowship is made up of young activists who are dedicated to creating a better world for wolves and other wildlife. Members range in age from eight to sixteen years. They have held coyote-awareness puppet shows to promote coexisting with carnivores, created websites to spread the word about endangered species, and competed in many science fairs with projects that emphasize the role wolves play in the environment. One member, Lizzy, wrote a short story describing the devastating aerial hunting of wolves in British Columbia. She also ran a 5K race to raise money for the WCC. This is a pack that really works together!

LEGACY

A month after I visited the wolves at the Wolf Conservation Center, I was sitting in an Adirondack chair overlooking majestic Lake George in northern New York, rereading a book by Barry Lopez called *Of Wolves and Men*. It was a sunny spring morning, birds were singing, and I wondered how it must have been to hear the howl of a wolf in the evenings here. It made me sentimental for things gone from these parts, and I wished the 1990s campaign to reintroduce wolves to the Adirondack Park had been as successful as their reintroduction to Yellowstone.

Lopez wrote about why wolves have been killed over the centuries: "Wolf killing goes beyond predator control, of course. Bounty hunters kill wolves for money; trappers kill them for pelts; scientists kill them for data; big game hunters kill them for trophies."

But he goes on to explain that wolves have not only been systematically killed, they have been tortured—set on fire, had their Achilles tendons cut, and poisoned. This goes beyond the need to protect livestock and family. This stems from deep-rooted fear and hatred.

Even as I wrote this book, wolf eradication headlines screamed out from the news. And not only in the United States. Norway decided to kill 70 percent of its wolf population amid protests. Hunters in Finland were authorized to kill 20 percent of their wolves.

Will collisions with wolves end in their mortality or can we learn to coexist with them?

But there is good news out there too—gray wolves have survived beyond the brink of extinction, and in Romania, trophy hunting of wolves was recently outlawed.

We can all hope that all these negative feelings can be put aside before the result is irreversible. And then, perhaps, one day I will sit in this very spot and hear the howl of a wild wolf.

BALD EAGLES FLY HIGH

OUR NATIONAL BIRD

I'm sitting aboard a train, riding north along the majestic ice-rimmed Hudson River in New York State. I stare out the window and gasp at the sight of a bald eagle (*Haliaeetus leucocephalus*), its wings spread, flying parallel to the train.

I want to stand up and shout, "Hey, everyone. Look—there's an eagle!" But instead I sit mesmerized, my heart beating in rhythm with each flap of the powerful wings. The white-headed bird flies above the open water until it is out of sight.

Decades ago the population of bald eagles in New York State dwindled from more than seventy nesting pairs to a single unproductive nesting pair living on a small lake in the Finger Lakes region—Hemlock Lake. Just one pair in the entire state! And across the country the news was equally dismal. America's national bird, our symbol of strength and courage, was in danger of becoming extinct.

America's Bicentennial celebrations in 1976 marked an important moment in our country's history. Special coins were minted, fireworks launched, parades planned. Tall ships sailed into America's harbors. The

Bald eagles are not really bald. Their heads are covered with white feathers.

country was celebrating all things American. But across all those festivities a shadow loomed. If we didn't act soon, the bird that graced the Great Seal of the United States would be lost forever.

Just ten days after the country's big birthday, the U.S. Department of the Interior's Fish and Wildlife Service announced that the bald eagle had been proposed for the Endangered Species List. It took two more years, but the eagle was finally listed in 1978.

Why had this population decreased so drastically? After all, bald eagles don't have many predators. What was killing them?

PESTICIDE KILLS EAGLES

It turned out that *we* were—directly and indirectly.

In the first half of the twentieth century, more than a hundred thousand bald eagles were shot and killed in Alaska by fishermen who feared that these birds were a threat to the salmon population. In addition, oil spills, loss of habitat, collisions with utility poles, and lead poisoning from lead fishing sinkers were also blamed for the eagle population's decline.

But something else sent this population into a nosedive. In the years after World War II, a pesticide called DDT (Dichlorodiphenyltrichloroethane) was used to kill agricultural pests. It turned out to be a deadly chemical. Rachel Carson wrote about the dangers of DDT and other pesticides in her famous book *Silent Spring,* published in 1962. The widespread use of poisonous pesticides was far-reaching. Not only did it kill insects and thereby have an impact on all creatures that relied on insects for food, it was also carried right through the food chain—even to the fish eaten by bald eagles and other birds, like osprey.

When the pesticide was sprayed, it landed on plants, on trees, and on the ground. It seeped into groundwater. It leaked into wetlands. Infected fish were eaten by many birds, not just by bald eagles. The DDT didn't kill the eagles directly; it disrupted their endocrine system and caused their egg-shells to be too thin to support the chicks growing inside them. The newly laid eggs were crushed under the weight of the mother bird's body.

Eagles' claws are called *talons*. Talons, unlike other animals' claws, are designed to allow eagles to carry large things, like fish.

RECOVERY BEGINS

New York State led the way for the nationwide recovery of bald eagles. This program to restore our national bird began in 1976, the year of America's Bicentennial.

Bald eagles, like many birds, mate for life. A pair selects a nesting territory and uses it for the rest of their lives. And that's a long time—eagles can live more than thirty years in the wild. Native to North America, they inhabit every state except Hawaii, and they are also found in Canada. They prefer to live near water.

These traits have helped and harmed their recovery.

THE BALD EAGLE ACT OF 1940

During the 1930s, people started to notice that the bald eagle population was decreasing. The Bald Eagle Protection Act was passed to protect the eagles from harassment by humans. It prohibited "the taking, possession and commerce" of bald and golden eagles. This gave the eagle population a little time to recover, but then the use of DDT and other pesticides began.

Take a look at how the Bald Eagle Protection Act was amended by Congress in 1959, 1962, 1972, and 1978. It was strengthened in 1972 with stricter penalties, but weakened in 1978. These actions demonstrate the importance of being vigilant with all our legislation, even after it is initially passed.

Bald eagles will nest where they can easily find food. This American bald eagle has built a nest atop a cell phone tower near the ocean.

NEW YORK STATE EAGLE RECOVERY PROJECT

DDT was banned in 1972, but no one knew how much lingered in the environment. How would scientists erase the damage it had done? Could they find a DDT-free site for their bald eagle recovery program?

Biologists explored a process based on the idea that when eagles breed, they return to the habitat where they were hatched. If juvenile birds could be brought in from other states and released in New York, would they return there to breed? Would the eagles return to the place where they hatched or where they first learned to fly? The scientists hoped they would return to their adopted New York home.

But there were more questions to explore.

How would the young eagles learn to hunt without eagle parents to teach them?

HACKING

The New York State Department of Environmental Conservation (DEC) set out to answer those questions. Looking at the hacking programs that had been used for falcons, the DEC biologists developed a plan for bald eagles.

Hacking is a process where young eagles, called eaglets, are placed on a manmade nesting platform, called a hacking tower, for several weeks before they leave the nest, or fledge. Human caretakers feed and care for the young birds from behind a blind or an enclosure within the tower so that the birds do not have any human interaction.

Fortunately, the New York State DEC found a DDT-free site at the Montezuma National Wildlife Refuge in central New York, where they established the world's first bald eagle hacking towers. They set up two hacking towers, each with two compartments.

The first two eaglets arrived from Wisconsin in 1976. Others followed from Minnesota, Michigan, and Maryland, brought to the hacking site by DEC biologists. It was exciting and nerve-racking. Would the program work? Would the young eagles eventually fly from these towers and then return to the region to raise their own young?

Because the eaglets did not have eagle parents to feed them at this stage, human DEC caretakers fed and cared for them. George Steele, DEC wildlife technician for the Endangered Species Unit, worked onsite with the young birds, three days on and three days off. Eventually their feathers began to grow, and the birds started preparing to fledge, or fly away on their own.

When eaglets are twelve or thirteen weeks old, they are ready to start flying. Equipped with radio transmitters and wing markers, these young eagles began to be released.

"As the eagles grew their flight feathers, they would sometimes get airborne on windy days in their compartment," remembers George. "We'd

ECO-HERO: RACHEL CARSON

Rachel Carson had the vision to recognize the effects of pesticides on our entire environment. Her words did not resonate with everyone. Some claimed she was being hysterical. Many questioned her as a scientist. Others called her a Communist. And the pesticide industry was outraged by her claims. But others listened. President John F. Kennedy called for a committee to examine the effects of pesticides. The committee agreed with Carson. Her groundbreaking book led to the EPA ban on DDT in 1972 and helped launch the environmental movement.

creep in and quietly remove the caging around them and leave the compartment facing the marsh. The wind would gust up, and eventually they would fledge."

Even though the birds had left their nest, the technicians still left food there during the first week. As the days went on, the birds visited less and

EAGLE HACKING

Don't be confused. Hacking, in this case, has nothing to do with computers. It's actually an old term used to describe a method for training falcons. The term is derived from an Old English word for a wagon—a "hack"—that was used to house young falcons on a hillside before they were able to fly on their own.

New York State Department of Environmental Conservation's eagle hacking towers provided the perfect place to reintroduce eagles into the state.

less. Some days they would not visit, and the technicians knew they were eating on their own. But other days, when the eagles had a little trouble finding food, they could return to the safety of the hacking tower and get food there. After a couple of weeks the birds learned to catch fish or to find carcasses to feed on on their own.

An eagle arrives to be part of the New York DEC's hacking program.

SUCCESS?

During the first five years, the program released twenty-three bald eagles that were carefully monitored with transmitters. The wildlife biologists were thrilled that all those young eagles survived. They learned how to hunt and feed. They returned to the release site in the following years. But would they breed?

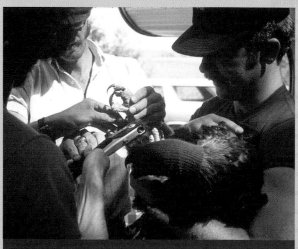

An American bald eagle is banded for identification so that it can be further monitored.

George Steele releases an eagle into the wild.

The program had a lot to celebrate, but soon there was even more to be happy about. In 1980, two of the eagles released were found nesting in a spot about two hours away. The pair hatched two chicks and fledged one. Success!

The DEC moved on to the next phase, with the goal of restoring ten nesting pairs to New York. They built three hacking tower condos, larger than the original towers, providing enough space for about 175 birds over a nine-year period in three locations within the state—Iroquois National Wildlife Refuge, Adirondack Park, and Alcove Reservoir. Each site could hold twenty eagles at a time.

The program was soaring!

RESTORATION

Although the New York State hacking program ended in 1989, the bald eagle population is still carefully monitored. Over the course of the program, 198 eagles were successfully released. Habitat lands have been acquired and protected, thanks to the state's Environmental Protection Fund and Environmental Quality Bond Act.

"New York has been a leader in the restoration and recovery of the bald eagle in the Northeast," New York DEC commissioner Basil Seggos said. "The DEC recently confirmed that New York has been home to the longest-living wild bald eagle on record in the United States and that bald eagles are now nesting all across the state. The restoration of the bald eagle, the symbol of our nation, confirms that New York's rivers, lakes, and forests have made a tremendous comeback. New York's ongoing recovery efforts will help ensure a healthy bald eagle population in the state."

A wonderful sight—an immature bald eagle perched in the wild in New York State. It takes five years for a bald eagle to attain its iconic solid white head and tail feathers.

The biologists who worked on the restoration have taken its success very personally. Pete Nye, for example. He ran the DEC's Endangered Species Unit, and eagles were his main project.

"Eagles were the one thing I kept tenaciously for myself, and as a biologist, that's what makes it all worthwhile," he said. He started at age twenty-six and was still studying eagles when he retired at sixty.

The eagle biologists celebrated each release and each milestone. There are now more than 220 nesting pairs in New York. "That makes me as proud as anything I've done in my life," said Pete.

George Steele read about the death of the oldest wild bald eagle and knew by its leg band that it was one he had helped band in 1977. He mourned its loss but celebrated the life that he had helped into the world. That eagle not only lived a long life, he left behind his young to—as Steele said—"soar in the skies of New York."

NATIONAL SUCCESS

Bald eagles were officially delisted on June 28, 2007, based on estimates of close to ten thousand nesting pairs living in the Lower 48 states. Bald eagle protection is still in place, even though the species is no longer deemed endangered. Our national bird is protected under the Migratory Bird Treaty Act of 1918 and the Bald Eagle Protection Act of

Signs on New York hiking trails warn hikers not to disturb nesting bald eagles.

1940. Both laws prohibit people from killing, selling, or harming bald or golden eagles. It also protects their nests and eggs.

But Pete Nye reminds us that the future is not guaranteed.

"I feel pretty good that eagles are going to be fine in the short term," he said. But he's concerned that they might not be able to continue to live and breed in the places they inhabit today. Human disturbance can reverse the progress.

ICE ON THE HUDSON

Sitting on the train, as I gaze out over the river beyond the railroad tracks, ice chunks line the shore and ice cutters have carved out channels of open water a bit farther out. That is where the eagles are searching for their next meal. I can no longer see the eagle that flew beside my window, just the frozen landscape. I scan the area, hoping to get one more glance at that mighty bird, but it isn't really necessary. That one moment will stay with me forever—a testament to the extraordinary efforts that have restored the eagle population.

An eagle pair builds their substantial twig nest in a tree near the Hudson River. Scientists continue to monitor all nesting pairs.

PESTICIDES AND PELICANS

Eagles were not the only bird affected by pesticides from the 1950s to the early 1970s, when those pesticides were finally banned. Brown pelicans lived in estuaries and marine habitats along the East and West coasts, all the way from California to the Carolinas. Pelicans forage for small fish that swim in schools in coastal waters and even farther offshore, scooping them up in their dip-net bills. Then they started to disappear. By 1963, the only pelicans in Louisiana were the ones on the state flag. And in the late 1960s pelican colonies in Southern California shrank by more than 90 percent. Pesticide use caused the decline of both populations. In Louisiana, a pesticide called Endrin killed fish in the estuaries and then killed the pelicans. In Los Angeles a chemical plant released thousands of pounds of DDT into the sewer system. It entered the ocean and was absorbed by the fish that the pelicans ate. The California pelicans didn't die directly from the pesticide, as the Louisiana birds did, but the chemical altered the way the birds processed calcium, causing them to lay eggs with thinner shells—just like the eagles.

And scientists, as they did with the eagles, used the method of transplanting the young to recover the pelican population. Thanks to the dedicated efforts of conservationists, pelican populations are on the rise.

Brown pelicans (*Pelecanus occidentalis*), another shorebird that suffered from pesticide poisoning, have rebounded thanks to scientists!

Brown pelicans can eat roughly four pounds of fish a day.

Tortoises' closest relatives are birds and crocodiles, not snakes and lizards as you might think.

GIANT GALÁPAGOS TORTOISES WALK THE EARTH

ARRIVAL

Our plane approaches the tiny island of Baltra in the Galápagos and, looking out my window, I see a few of the other nineteen islands poking up out of the vast blue Pacific Ocean. I imagine myself as an ancient explorer, sailing to these islands and seeing them for the first time. As wonderstruck as I am, I can only imagine how magnificent they must have been to those early sailors who were greeted by never-before-seen birds flying overhead and wild creatures on the coastline.

And somewhere below me are the famed tortoises that these islands are named after. Galápagos is an Old Spanish word for tortoise. Soon I will be able to see them for myself.

Before we put up our tray tables, instructions come over the speakers, shaking me out of my daydream. We are preparing for our descent, and we can't get there fast enough for my liking.

The island is a vast desert until we reach the ferry to Santa Cruz. Lava rocks and cacti fill the landscape, and heat pours in through the open bus windows. It is not the Eden I imagined, that is, not until the bus reaches the shoreline and the first signs of life pass before our eyes. Red crabs dot the black rocks, and birds with fantastical feather tails and prehistoric-looking beaks swoop over and near the ferry. Eager visitors clamber aboard to take their seats. Cameras emerge. There is something new to see in every direction. It reminds me of the movie *Jurassic Park*, except this is real. But where are the tortoises?

We dock ten minutes later, and our guide, Wilson, places our luggage in the back of his official white pickup truck for our trip into the highlands of Santa Cruz, where the tortoises live. The island changes from desert to forest as we drive past mossy scalesia trees. We pass ancient craters, avocado trees, coffee plantations, and cows. Finally Wilson stops at a private farm

GETTING THERE

The island Baltra hosts the airport for the larger island of Santa Cruz, or Indefatigable, as it was once known. It is one of only two Galápagos islands that offer air service. Flights to the Galápagos leave from Quito or Guayaquil in Ecuador and land on either Baltra or San Cristóbal Island. It is very important that visitors are not carrying any invasive species with them that could damage the islands, so everyone must pass through special security. The overhead bins on the plane are sprayed with insecticide before we are allowed to exit the plane, and a specially treated carpet makes sure that there is nothing harmful on the soles of our shoes. Suitcases and bags are triple-checked. Any food or fruit is confiscated. After we are finally cleared to enter the islands, we board a bus to the ferry that will carry us to Santa Cruz.

whose owners earn part of their income by allowing tourists to see the tortoises that have called this land theirs for eternity.

After years of dreaming about this place, three flights, and an overnight stay, I will finally get to see the tortoises.

MEET THE TORTOISES

Without so much as a glance we rush past the small gazebo housing a collection of tortoise skulls, bones, and shells to get to the main attraction: a huge Galápagos tortoise (*Chelonoidis donfaustoi*) rests just feet away, munching on the grass. A group of tourists excitedly stands around it. It's late afternoon, and the sunlight bounces off the creature's worn, mud-covered carapace.

I spy another tortoise munching away in the opposite direction. It's by itself, with no tourists around. I walk over and crouch beside it, close enough to hear it breathing—deep, low, almost prehistoric breaths. As I look into its eyes, I wonder how many other human faces it has gazed back at over the years: sailors, farmers, scientists, and tourists.

A tortoise's top shell is called the *carapace;* the bottom shell is the *plastron.* Galápagos tortoises have a saddleback-shaped shell if they live on dry islands or a domed shell if they live in areas with more lush vegetation, like the highlands of Santa Cruz.

Although tortoises spend a lot of time in muddy pools to protect themselves from parasites and biting insects, they can go months without drinking any water.

These tortoises can live far longer than we humans can. They reach their hundredth birthday and just keep going. Tortoises can live to be 170 years old. The Galápagos tortoise that died in 2006 at Steve Irwin's Australia Zoo was originally owned by Charles Darwin himself in 1835. Do the math!

HISTORY

When the first Europeans arrived on the islands in 1535, long before Darwin, they found these creatures "foolishly tame," many of them having never encountered a predator until that time. This was a boon for visitors, but not very good for the tortoises. Early whalers and pirates left their mark, and today the islands have faced pollution, overpopulation, illegal fishing, alien species, climate change, and mass tourism. All these factors have affected the ecosystems of the islands and the population of its tortoises and other wild residents.

Wilson hurries us down the path as the sun is setting. This is the equator.

The sun rises at six a.m. and sets twelve hours later. I could have sat beside this giant creature all day, but I am hoping there are more to see. We follow Wilson, stepping gingerly over sharp red lava rocks and branches. I can't stop myself from looking to either side of the path. To the right I see another huge shell, wedged between some branches in the undergrowth. To the left is a puddle, with four tortoises partly submerged in the mud that protects them from parasites and cools them. Even Wilson pauses for a moment at the sight of them. But not for long. He keeps us moving until we reach a much larger muddy spot where several tortoises are spending the late afternoon. Tiny sunshine-yellow canaries flit in and out of the mucky edges.

LIMITED TOURISM

Even though tourists arrive on commercial flights every day, these islands are not a typical vacation destination. About six hundred miles off the coast of Ecuador, the Galápagos Islands are home to unique animals and they have special national park designation. In fact, only four of the islands are inhabited. You can't just step off the plane and begin your vacation the way you can on other islands. You have to fill out an endless number of forms and go through numerous checkpoints—all for good reason. The Galápagos began scaling back tourism in the 1960s. The number of tourist boats now operating is limited to just over eighty, and their maximum number of passengers is one hundred. You won't see large cruise ships here. There's also a cap on the number of hotel beds on the island, as well as onshore visits. Touring vessels are allowed to visit an island site only once every fifteen days and are assigned a time slot, all to limit the number of humans treading on sensitive island ecosystems.

DARWIN AND THE *BEAGLE* NOTEBOOKS

Although Charles Darwin was certainly not the first person to investigate these islands, they became forever linked to his theory of evolution when his voyage on the *Beagle* inspired his writing of *On the Origin of Species*.

"The tortoise is very fond of water, drinking large quantities, and wallowing in the mud," he wrote. He goes on to say that the vice governor of the colony, Mr. Lawson, spoke of tortoises so large that sometimes six or eight men were required to lift them.

That's certainly believable, as the ones in front of me look like boulders.

When tortoises do drink, they will drink large amounts that are then stored in their bladder and the root of their neck, the pericardium. This characteristic was another reason why sailors found them useful.

POPULATION PLUMMETS

All the creatures on the islands have been affected by humans, but none is as well known as the giant tortoise. These tortoises once lived in many other parts of the world, but today they survive only here on these Ecuadorian islands and in a group of islands in the Indian Ocean called the Aldabra Atoll.

Not only are they a marvel because of their size and longevity, they are also crucial members of their ecosystems. Long-necked Galápagos tortoises on the island of Española, for example, eat the fruits and pads of island cacti, thereby distributing those seeds across the island through their droppings. The cacti are known as a keystone species, providing food for lots of other creatures, such as finches, mockingbirds, and lizards. The tortoises support the cacti population.

Unfortunately, early sailors, pirates, and whalers found these slow-moving tortoises a perfect food source for themselves.

"The meat of this animal is the easiest of digestion, and a quantity of it, exceeding that of any other food, can be eaten without experiencing the slightest inconvenience. But what seems the most extraordinary in this animal, is the length of time that it can exist without food." This was written by Captain David Porter of the U.S. Navy in his journal. Captain Porter sailed on the frigate USS *Essex* in 1812, 1813, and 1814.

They found that they could capture and stash hundreds of tortoises in the holds of their ships without having to feed them, using them for food as they sailed. Tortoises could last a year and a half upside down in the ships' holds, enabling the sailors to have fresh meat as they needed it. This was a heartbreaking and cruel fate for many.

Even Darwin wrote of eating tortoise meat in his notes from the *Beagle*: "The people employ the meat largely, eating it both fresh & salt, & it is very good.—The meat abounds with yellow fat, which is fried down & gives a beautifully clear & good oil."

ALIEN PREDATORS

These huge armored creatures (the males weigh about 600 pounds, or 272 kg), have faced another threat: goats! Early sailors introduced goats to the islands, and the goats ate vital tortoise habitat. Tortoises rely on forests for shade, food, and water. Before the goats, the island of Isabela had an impenetrable forest. Even in the dry season a thick mist would move onto the island, catch in the branches of the trees, and drip down into pools that the tortoises loved to soak in.

But the goats changed that. As they multiplied, they destroyed forests. That meant no drip pools, no shade. More than a hundred thousand goats ate entire forests on many of the islands, including Isabela, decimating the island's tortoise population, turning the land into something of a dustbowl.

It was impossible for the tortoises to survive both the goats and the sailors. These creatures even faced egg-eating rats brought to the islands centuries before. It is no surprise that the Galápagos tortoises were brought to the brink of extinction on many islands.

In his book *Galápagos: World's End*, William Beebe quoted R. H. Beck's account of the demise of the tortoises that appeared in the New York Zoological Society's 1905 report: "It is only within the last few years that the home of these very large tortoises has been invaded by man, but the rapidity with which they are being killed, and the reason for their destruction, leaves us but little hope that they all survive any longer

REARING LONESOME GEORGE'S SPECIES

The solo Pinta Island tortoise, affectionately called Lonesome George, died in June 2012. Although scientists had tried for years to breed him, they were unsuccessful. But perhaps his fate won't be that of his species. Although it was believed that he was the very last *Chelonoidis abingdonii* tortoise, scientists have found genes of this species in tortoises on other islands. They believe that, centuries ago, sailors dropped off Pinta Island tortoises on other islands in the Galápagos, where they mated with the local tortoise species. The resulting generations of offspring carried a little bit of their Pinta Island ancestors with them. Although there is not another tortoise that is 100 percent genetically similar to George, it might be possible to breed two tortoises that both have some Pinta Island genes in order to obtain offspring that are more closely related to him genetically. Conservationists are hopeful that, over a number of years and generations, they may obtain a Pinta Island tortoise—*Chelonoidis abingdonii*—again.

Galápagos tortoises have been known to live over 170 years.

than did the American bison after the hide hunters began their work of extermination."

There were fifteen giant tortoises left on the southeastern Galápagos island of Española by the 1960s.

Fifteen.

GOATS AND TORTOISES

It's somewhat of a miracle that I am able to see so many tortoises on this trip. It took drastic measures, soul-searching, and the work of dedicated conservationists to assure that all the treasured Galápagos tortoises would not become extinct. The motivation for such drastic measures was supported by the belief that if you break something, you must fix it. We had caused the problem, so we needed to rectify it.

TORTOISE EVOLUTION LEADS TO ISLAND VARIETY

Darwin noticed that each island's tortoises were different, writing that "slight variations in the form of the shell are constant according to the Island which they inhabit—also the average largest size appears equally to vary according to the locality."

There are many different species of tortoises living on the islands today. Fifteen, to be exact. And that number is still changing. Just recently a new species was found on the island of Santa Cruz. Why so many? For the same reason that there are different varieties of finches on the islands. It's called *adaptive radiation*. This phenomenon is caused by many years of isolation and the competition faced by each species of wildlife.

Naturalists in the nineteenth century held two competing beliefs. One group believed that the giant land tortoises formed many unique species, each classified by its island habitat and its shell shape. The other group believed that despite the variety found among the tortoises, they all belonged under the same species, *Chelonoidis nigra*. Today, researchers mainly agree that there are different tortoise species, all under the genus *Chelonoidis*.

Even on the same island there can be different species. On Santa Cruz there is a group of about 250 tortoises living just twelve miles away from another group of about 3,000. The smaller eastern group can be distinguished from their island cousins by their diminutive size and their slightly different shell shape. DNA tests have shown that these two groups are as different as species living on two separate islands. Named after Fausto Llerena Sánchez, Ecuador's oldest park ranger, the new species recently identified on Santa Cruz is known as *C. donfaustoi*.

Let's look at one island in particular. For centuries, the goats stayed on one side of Isabela Island, unable to cross the sharp natural lava rock barrier. The tortoises lived happily on the other side. But in the 1970s something changed. The goats began to cross over. Soon goats and tortoises were fighting for the same habitat. In only about twenty years, the one hundred thousand goats on the island were eating just about everything they could.

Islanders had to examine how they would handle these goats, which had been on the islands since the first sailors arrived—some five hundred years earlier. They weren't just some annoying invasive species, such as the kudzu vines from Japan that entered the United States and can grow about a foot a day. These were animals that had become part of the history and culture of the islands. They were an additional food source for locals, and visitors enjoyed seeing them in the landscape. But at what price? They were destroying the ecosystem, including the tortoise population. Conservationists had to make some harsh decisions. Was the answer to kill one species to save another? Time and again, this is the question facing scientists and conservationists. In this case, it was pretty clear. The goats were an introduced species. They were not endemic to the islands, and sadly, they would have to be exterminated to restore the islands. If officials didn't get rid of the goats, the entire ecosystem would continue to collapse.

A tortoise summit was held in 1995 in the United Kingdom. Scientists and other interested parties arrived to brainstorm about what could be done. They investigated each idea, including bringing lions to the island to prey on the goats.

They concluded that the Galápagos National Park Service would institute a monumental goat hunt on Isabela Island to begin the land's restoration. They hired New Zealand pilot and sharpshooter Fraser Sutherland and four helicopters to follow the goats and shoot them. It was a desperate but realistic measure. They called this Project Isabela. They successfully killed about 90 percent of the goats, but some escaped. The ones that survived became better educated and hid at the sound of the helicopters. As we know, nature always finds a way to survive. Of course, these goats had young that also evaded the helicopters. The population of smarter goats grew. Now what?

Scientists have found that about forty-five Santa Cruz island plants spread their seeds through tortoise scat. Each piece of scat could contain hundreds of tiny seeds.

JUDAS GOATS

The scientists employed what became known as "Judas goats." They would capture goats, put radio collars on them, and release them again on the island. The collared goats would unknowingly lead the scientists to the hiding goats. The scientists would then shoot all the hidden goats, spare the collared goat, and continue the process every two weeks for a year. This was successful until the collared goat became pregnant. Now what?

The scientists sterilized the collared goat and rereleased it on the island. Finally they had success! They ended up eliminating 250,000 of the destructive goats.

With the goats gone, the ecosystem began to return to its pre-human, pre-goat condition. Plants and trees grew back. The drip pools returned. And, most important, the tortoise population began to thrive again.

The tortoises are even helping the ecosystem return to its pre-goat state by trampling the woody plants that sprout up. They also eat cactus and spread its seeds. The process might take centuries before the island completely recovers, but it is moving forward.

JUDAS ANIMALS

Judas animals, named after the famous biblical Apostle, are members of an unwanted invasive species that are used to hunt others of their kind that are destroying native biodiversity. Aside from goats in the Galápagos, scientists have used this practice to rid the Florida Everglades of damaging Burmese pythons and feral pigs.

FISHERMEN REVOLT

Not everyone on the island supported tortoise recovery efforts. When the fishermen received National Park Service fishing regulations that had an impact on their livelihoods, they struck out against the park by releasing goats back to the island to disrupt the project. They even killed tortoises and attacked rangers! Thankfully, the fishermen have since transitioned to earning their living from tourism, and the tortoises are safer.

MOBY DICK AUTHOR HERMAN MELVILLE MEETS THE TORTOISES

Many famous people have visited the islands and witnessed the majesty of the Galápagos tortoises, including Herman Melville, the author of *Moby Dick*. He wrote about seeing these unique reptiles,

> But instead of three custom-house officers, behold these really wondrous tortoises—none of your schoolboy mud-turtles—but black as widower's weeds, heavy as chests of plate, with vast shells medallioned and orbed like shields, and dented and blistered like shields that have breasted a battle—shaggy too, here and there, with dark green moss, and slimy spray of sea. These mystic creatures, suddenly translated by night from unutterable solitudes to our peopled deck, affected me in a manner not easy to unfold. They seem newly crawled forth from beneath the foundations of the world. Yea, they seemed the identical tortoises whereon the Hindoo plants this total sphere. With a lantern I inspected them more closely. Such worshipful venerableness of aspect! Such furry greenness mantling the rude peelings and hearing the fissures of their shattered shells. I no more saw three tortoises. They expanded—became transfigured. I seemed to see three Roman Coliseums in magnificent decay.

SCIENCE CONTINUES

The recovery of the Galápagos tortoise is far from over, but it certainly has brought the tortoises back from the brink of extinction. Even so, there is still much to be done. Scientists continue their studies on the islands and continue breeding these ancient reptiles.

The island fox (*Urocoyon littorals*) is found only on the Channel Islands, off the coast of southern California.

November 2016 began with the first survey on the island of San Cristóbal of one of the least-known Galápagos tortoise species, *Chelonidis chathamensis*. This important census recorded the number of tortoises found, their sex, their age, and their health condition. Scientists will be able to use the information to ensure the health of this species and its island habitat.

I wish I could stay on the Galápagos to explore each island and see each tortoise species. The beauty and uniqueness are beyond measure, and I find it hard to say goodbye when it comes time to leave. As the boat ferries us to Baltra, I look back at the highlands behind us with the knowledge that the tortoises will safely live another day to look into someone else's eyes.

CALIFORNIA'S ISLAND FOXES REBOUND!

The Galápagos tortoises are not the only islanders threatened by an invasive species brought to their habitat by man. We can look to California's Channel Islands for a similar story. In this case, island foxes were on the losing end. Feral pigs, brought to the islands in the mid-nineteenth century, attracted flocks of golden eagles. The golden eagles had an easy time. The competitive bald eagle population had been hit by DDT poisoning, enabling the golden eagles to take over the island and prey on the foxes. The fox population plummeted. By 1999, there were only about fifteen foxes left on Santa Rosa and also on San Miguel. Conservationists and concerned citizens jumped into action. A breeding program was set up, and the pigs, like the Galápagos goats, were killed. Golden eagles were moved and bald eagles were released. More than two hundred foxes were released into the wild. In August 2016, the foxes were removed from protection under the Endangered Species Act and declared a success story.

CALIFORNIA CONDORS SOAR AGAIN

SEARCHING THE SKIES

Morning fog rises above jagged mountains as I meet Nadya Seal Faith in a parking lot in Fillmore, California. Nadya is a California condor nest technician, and the mountainous landscape of Los Padres National Forest is her office. Somewhere among the crags and stony cliffs of those mountains live California condors (*Gymnogyps californianus*).

Nadya is going to be my guide in condor country. To begin our adventure, I eagerly place my backpack with my camera, binoculars, and notebook on the floor of her Land Rover. As she starts driving up the mountain, along roads that are not open to the public, I'm thankful that I'm not behind the wheel. The narrow, winding pavement has turned to dirt and dust. We bounce along slowly, climbing higher and higher, our movements not nearly as smooth and graceful as the large-winged vultures who can once again make this ascent effortlessly, thanks to dedicated conservationists who have worked tirelessly to help this species recover from the brink of extinction.

Have you ever seen a vulture soar in the sky above you? It's big, right? It's hard to believe a bird could be larger. But you probably haven't seen a

The bald head that all condors have is an adaptation that enables them to feed more easily on the remains of dead animals, called *carrion*.

The dirt roads leading into the condor habitat are traveled daily by researchers working on condor recovery.

California condor. These majestic birds are the largest soaring birds in continental North America. From wingtip to wingtip they can reach nine or ten feet. I'm just over five feet tall, so that is double my height. It's hard to mistake a California condor when you see one soaring up above you, its wings spread into the wind.

I am hoping to catch a glimpse of one today, knowing it was only decades ago that we risked losing California condors forever due to the loss of habitat and food sources and to poisoning, collecting, and shooting deaths. Seeing one now is something that would never have been possible without the conservationists who made the difficult decision decades ago to begin a controversial recovery program.

FROM ROYALTY TO ENDANGERED

It wasn't until 1833 that these giant prehistoric birds became known as California condors. Before that they were called California vultures or Royal vultures. Once, a long time ago, they did rule the skies, so the use of the word *royal* wasn't inaccurate. Condor skeletons have been extracted from the La Brea Tar Pits. These birds once flew above saber-toothed tigers in Pleistocene-era California. Fossils show that they even flew over land that is now New York and Florida. That was about ten thousand years ago; now it is hard to recall a time when the condor population has not been struggling. There have been lots of factors that hurt the population. Condors were shot for their feathers; they often flew into manmade structures, such as power poles; but mostly, the birds suffered from lead poisoning. The population decreased to such a low number that the condor was listed as endangered in 1967.

Condor road signs alert drivers to birds that might fly down for a meal.

Although there are about 260 condors now in the wild, their population is not fully recovered and continues to be threatened. Like their vulture relatives, California condors are scavenger birds. They eat what is left over, the dead carrion that is forgotten after predators, including humans, have had their fill. As nature's cleaner-uppers, they often end up eating food that isn't healthy for them. Hunters often leave behind carcasses filled with lead shot from their guns, and condors eat those carcasses. Lead poisoning is the main reason why their population has not fully recovered. Condors can fly more than a hundred miles each day, finding food in all sorts of places, including livestock and hunting ranches. Many of these carcasses contain lead.

All the condors in the wild today, both captive reared and fledged in the wild, suffer from some level of lead poisoning owing to the ingestion of lead-filled carrion. Lead is absorbed in the digestive tract and ultimately, if not treated, creates a paralysis that causes a condor's digestive system to stop working. When lead levels become high, untreated birds die of starvation. The extent of the poisoning determines whether or not they will survive.

Lead might be the main cause, but it is not the only problem threatening their survival. They also eat the trash that humans carelessly leave behind,

CALIFORNIA CONDOR RECOVERY PLAN GOALS

1. Establish a captive breeding program—this began in 1982.

2. Reintroduce California condors into the wild.

3. Minimize mortality factors.

4. Maintain condor habitat.

5. Implement information and educational programs.

such as bottle caps, glass, nuts and bolts, and plastic. They mistake these tiny objects, called *microtrash,* for small rocks that would aid in digestion or bits of bone that can supply a chick with needed calcium. Condor parents can't tell the difference and can be seen on webcams feeding these objects to their nestlings. Not only can microtrash cause internal cuts and bleeding, it can become lodged in a young bird's digestive system, leaving it unable to digest food and eventually causing it to die of starvation.

CONTROVERSIAL CAPTURE

Nadya and I are headed to the Hopper Mountain condor sanctuary within the Sespe Wilderness in Los Padres National Forest, where much of the condor recovery plan has taken place. Here young condors are being released and monitored, and previously released condors are raising families of their own.

The U.S. Fish and Wildlife Service Hopper Mountain National Wildlife Refuge Complex is the headquarters for the California Condor Recovery Program, which works with many partners to support condor recovery efforts.

The Sespe Wilderness area in Southern California encompasses 219,468 acres of jagged mountains and bouldered cliffs that make perfect nesting sites for condors. The Sespe Creek, the last undammed river in Southern California, runs through it. It is a wild area, dotted by the oil-drilling rigs manned by the Seneca Resources Corporation and a few power lines.

The Sespe was declared a wilderness area in 1992. It adheres to the Wilderness Act of 1964, which states that a wilderness area is "where earth and its community of life remain untrammeled, where man himself is a visitor who does not remain."

This is condor country! Those trees in the foreground provide the perfect perching spots for the large birds as they search the mountains and valleys for food.

Nadya points out a distant rocky hole on the side of a steep cliff—a condor nest site that has been used in the past. As thrilled as I am to see this, my heart sinks as I think back to the condor capture that occurred in these mountains in 1982. In May of that year a small California condor chick hatched in

On top of this rocky outcrop is a webcam used to view inside a condor nest, enabling scientists to monitor the health of a chick.

a similar cavity. His mother likely caressed his fluffy white body carefully with her massive beak, just as condors had been doing with their young for thousands of years. This rare, tiny, baldheaded chick, later named Xolxol (a native Chumash word meaning "one of the sky people," pronounced *ho-ho*), was taken by conservationists from his wild mother just months later to become the first member of a controversial breeding program that would change the course of the wild condor population forever.

It was a bittersweet moment for the scientists who captured Xolxol that August. Would their program succeed? The fate of the last wild condors rested squarely with them. Some felt that the few remaining condors should be left in the wild to soar the skies, even if that meant their extinction. Others felt that if the condors were all captured, there would be no justification for saving their mountainous habitat from development and drilling. But since their decline was caused by human beings, didn't they deserve our help to save them?

Xolxol's mom, named AC8 (Adult Condor 8) by scientists, became the

SPECIES ON THE EDGE

Scientists and politicians have to make very difficult decisions every day about endangered species and about how—or if—to attempt recovery efforts that can be expensive and possibly unsuccessful. Sometimes a species' recovery is determined by its "cute" factor and not whether it is a crucial member of an ecosystem. There are also species that have a worldwide concern. Scientists throughout the world often join forces to fight for the survival of a crucial species, sharing information and techniques that could be helpful in recovery efforts.

The Zoological Society of London has worked out a way to classify these species. It is called EDGE: Evolutionarily Distinct and Globally Endangered. The assigned EDGE number is derived from examining a species' lineage or history. The longer the evolutionary history and the fewer relatives the species has, the higher the Evolutionarily Distinct (ED) number. That number is then multiplied with another, called the Globally Endangered (GE) score, which indicates how endangered the species is around the planet, according to the international Red List. The more critically endangered the species is, the higher its GE score. The combined EDGE number is then ranked by scientists who have listed the species that have the highest EDGE scores. These species—often unusual in their genetic makeup and the way they look and behave—need our immediate and thoughtful protection.

California condors rank third on the list of globally endangered birds, just behind the New Caledonian owlet-nightjar and the giant ibis.

last free-flying condor captured for the breeding program. AC8 wasn't captured with Xolxol in 1982. She remained in the wild to breed, until she was the only wild female condor left. All the rest had perished from gunshot, lead poisoning, or microtrash impaction, or they'd been captured for the breeding program.

Although there were no other females in the wild, there were four males. Counting AC8, only *five* wild condors remained in the skies.

When AC8 and her mate were the last breeding pair left in the wild and the threat of lead poisoning loomed in their future, scientists decided it was time to capture all the rest of the wild condors. AC8, AC6, and AC2 were captured in 1986. Janet Hamber, a condor biologist and an archivist at the Santa Barbara Natural History Museum, had been monitoring AC2 for eleven years at eleven different nest sites. She watched as he was taken from the skies. With the help of a net cannon that releases a net into the air, where it opens and covers birds or animals without harming them.

The following year, AC5 was trapped. Zoologist Dr. Peter Bloom noticed AC9 watching him from a large oak as he placed AC5 into a kennel. AC9 was then the last remaining wild condor. For Peter, it was a glimpse of what it must have been like for the last dodo bird on earth. The condor sat by himself, his body dark against the setting sun. Peter, having studied AC9 in the wild for years, noted that he had always been a curious bird. "Even that day was spooky, really eerie, since AC9 hung around on a nearby tree and watched us take AC5 away," Peter said. "We've never had another condor stay around like that" during a capture.

On Easter Sunday in 1987, AC9 was captured with the use of a cannon that fired a net over him as he ate the remains of a stillborn calf set out as bait by scientists at the Bitter Creek National Wildlife Refuge.

For the first time in tens of thousands of years, the sky was devoid of any giant condors soaring over the canyons. All living condors, twenty-seven of them, were now in captivity. Janet, like all the scientists who took part in this historic experiment, did not know whether they would succeed or if they were dooming these last wild birds forever.

The zoos in Los Angeles and San Diego that housed the captive condors designed special aviaries for them. The plan was so controversial during those early years that the scientists sometimes stayed with the condors overnight to protect them from people who wanted to set them free. To many, the birds' freedom outweighed the possibility of the recovery of the species.

Xolxol went on to live at the San Diego Wild Animal Park. With his mate, AC37, he became the father of nineteen. He produced another nine eggs with AC45. Those offspring might never have been born if it wasn't for the condor recovery program. Xolxol still lives in San Diego with AC37.

WHAT HAPPENED TO AC8?

AC8, one of the oldest condors in the world, was released back into the wild in 2000. Unfortunately, three years after her release, she was illegally shot and killed while perched in a tree on Tejon Ranch during a company-sponsored pig hunt. As the genetic "founder bird," AC8 produced sixteen offspring and is the great-grandmother to all four of the Santa Barbara Zoo's condors.

FIELD NOTES

Janet Hamber wrote about witnessing that historic capture in her field notes: "I saw a puff of smoke and the net went over him just a foot or so from freedom . . . and I put my head on the steering wheel and cried for all the lost hopes, failed concepts, bitter in-fighting, lack of understanding, cruelty of the hunters, money hungry developers, and the loss of the great wild freedom those birds represented as well. I felt absolutely desolate. I went down to the trap site to help fold up the net and to see AC9 in the sky kennel, told him I was sorry . . . I just knew I had been part of an historic moment—the purposeful removing of an endangered species from the wild to save it . . . I can only hope captive breeding will work and the resolve to return condors to the skies of California will be maintained."

Spotting a California condor soaring in the sky is a breathtaking moment.

CONDOR NAMING

All condors are given ID numbers upon hatching. The early tags from the 1980s used the letters "AC" to represent Adult Condor. The number represents their parentage. The higher the number, the younger the bird. A color-coded tag is assigned with that number so that each condor can be tracked and monitored easily upon its release into the wild. Condor #518, for example, wears a black tag with her number—18. A black tag indicates that her number is in the 500s, so her official tag number is 518. Condor #326's tag is blue, with the number 26. The blue signifies that the number is in the 300s.

Black numbers on a white wing tag indicate which individual this is and make it easy to identify this condor when it is flying in the distance.

It's rewarding to stand atop a mountain today and know that the program those scientists began was successful, although the population is not fully recovered. My heart leaps as Nadya points out a stone cavity called nest OM15 (Oat Mountain 15). It's located on the side of a facing cliff, where a young condor was fledged just last year. The condor parents were equally extraordinary.

The hole in this rocky ledge has proven to be the perfect place to raise a condor chick.

The mom, #518, was a captive release, meaning she was born in captivity and then released successfully to the wild. The dad, #326, was fledged at Hopper Canyon without any intervention. Condor chicks began to hatch in the wild in 2002, marking a major milestone in the recovery.

Nadya finds nesting cavities by looking for bird droppings that appear as whitewash on the rocks, indicating where the condors are spending time, and by using radio telemetry to monitor the locations of condors of breeding age early in the nesting season. After a nest is located, Nadya and other biologists enter the nesting site to examine the egg, making sure that the embryo is alive and well. She holds the egg up to a warm bright light in a process called *candling,* which enables her to see the embryo inside. The eggs are also weighed.

Once a chick hatches, it is visited by a nest technician at 30, 60, 90, and 120 days old. Exams are given to make sure the chick is healthy. Unfortunately, sometimes there are nest failures—an egg doesn't hatch or a chick dies after birth. The recovery team will sometimes be able to replace the egg or the chick with one that is alive. If this is done early enough, the condor parents will accept the replacement as their own.

DOUBLE-CLUTCHING

Each female condor in a mating pair lays only one egg every two years. But scientists have learned that if they remove the first fertilized egg from a nest, the pair will mate again and lay another. The first egg can then be incubated in a lab or used to replace an egg that will not hatch.

Sometimes scientists swap out a real condor egg for a fake one if they believe it won't hatch.

THE JOB OF A NEST TECHNICIAN

A nest technician job offers the perfect blend of science and adventure. The condor nests Nadya monitors are as remote as you could imagine. She hikes into canyons and often rappels down rocky cliffs to reach the cavities where condors lay their eggs and rear their young.

The goal of her team is to locate every bird every day. Interns, such as Sandra Mayne, live at Hopper Mountain in shifts of ten days on and four days off. When on duty, they are out in the sanctuary taking signals three times a day with GPS trackers. Each bird receives a tag with a transmitter that has its own frequency when the bird reaches 120 days old. By listening to these signals, the team can tell if a bird is in a cavity, nesting, or out and about. The louder the beep, the closer the bird to the person doing the tracking. A consistent beep indicates that the bird is staying still and may be in a cavity. The results are logged each day, with abbreviations indicating the locations. For example, STOP is the abbreviation for Silver Tanks Observation Point.

Interns, like Sandra, stay at the research station and use telemetry to monitor the condor population.

Nadya takes out her transmitter. The skies over the mountains are clear and blue. And then we hear it—a beep. A condor! A moment later it comes into view, its large wings holding the wind below it as it soars high above the crags, rocks, and desert. I catch a glimpse of the yellow tag on its wing. Nadya passes me the scope; it's #237.

MICROTRASH

Nadya and I move inside the facility at Hopper Mountain. She sits down at a computer and begins to show me some footage from the webcams that monitor the cavities. She shows me a video of a parent condor feeding a bottle cap to a nestling. It's heartbreaking to watch, knowing you can't stop it.

Nadya and other nest technicians watch videos like this day after day. When they find a parent feeding its young a bottle cap or a piece of glass, they observe whether the nestling spits it out or attempts to swallow it. One of the ways to tell if the bird is suffering from an impaction is to watch the growth of its tail feathers. If the feathers are not growing, it might be necessary to remove the chick from the nest and surgically remove the object it swallowed. That's a nest technician's job. Nadya risks her own life to rescue chicks and deliver them to the Los Angeles Zoo, where the microtrash is surgically removed from young condors who have obstructions.

The careless littering of small objects, like bottle caps, is one of the main reasons why condor populations have not fully recovered.

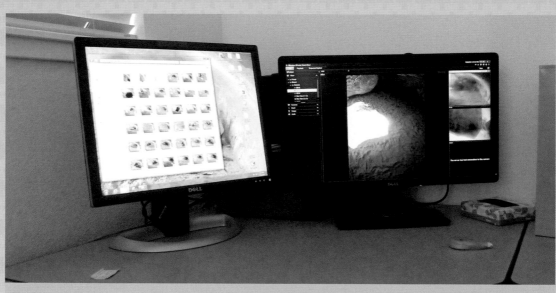

The Hopper Mountain station allows condor recovery teams to monitor condors in the wild and record their data without interfering with them unless absolutely necessary.

MICROTRASH AND SEA TURTLES

Microtrash isn't just a condor problem. Other species, such as sea turtles, also can suffer from impactions after ingesting our trash. The Sea Turtle Hospital in the Florida Keys treats endangered sea turtles suffering from impactions, many caused by natural objects like shells, but many more caused by balloons and other ocean debris. Impaction makes the turtles feel full, so they stop eating. Their treatment involves medicine, exercise, and rest.

Sea turtles also suffer from ingesting microtrash that ends up in the ocean.

TREATMENT

At the Los Angeles Zoo, condors have a team of dedicated animal keepers looking out for them. This team is there to treat birds that have impactions and lead poisoning. It's not what the team started out to do. Their original mission was captive breeding, but more and more of their time is focused on treating the released and wild birds.

After leaving Nadya, the mountains, and the free-flying condors, I drive about a hundred miles south to Los Angeles to visit the team at the LA Zoo.

During my visit, five condors are being treated for elevated lead levels. These five were part of a group of seventeen that were recently tested during a routine health check. The lead levels in the others were low enough

GET THE LEAD OUT

The Center for Biological Diversity's Get the Lead Out campaign asks the question, How many times should a bullet kill? Lead, an extremely toxic chemical to all animal life, continues to enter the food chain through the use of lead hunting ammunition and fishing tackle. It not only poisons wildlife, such as the California condor, it also threatens the health of humans. Scientists have found ammunition within condor digestive tracts and also found deer carcasses in condor range contaminated with lead from ammunition used in hunting. It has been found that lead is responsible for poisoning at least seventy-five wild bird species in the United States. On President Obama's last day in office, the U.S. Fish and Wildlife Service issued an order phasing out the use of lead ammunition on national wildlife refuges by 2022. However, this phaseout was reversed by President Donald Trump's appointee, Interior Secretary Ryan Zinke, on his first day in office less than three months later.

This adult condor, undergoing treatment for lead poisoning at the LA Zoo, will be released back into the wild when it is healthy again.

so that they did not need immediate care. But even with only five needing treatment, the animal keepers have their hands full.

Condors undergo a process/treatment called *chelation* to reduce the amount of lead in their blood. To see if treatment is necessary, the animal keepers perform tests that measure the amount of lead in a condor's blood and feathers. A bird needing therapy has 450 ng/ml (nanograms per milliliter) of lead in its blood. Sometimes a condor is busy parenting a nestling at the same time that it needs care. In that case the affected adult is brought in for treatment, and the other parent remains to care for the chick. The length of time of treatment varies with the severity of the poisoning. In moderate cases treatment could take weeks or months. For some birds with higher levels of lead, treatments have taken a year.

The chelation treatment process for each bird is tedious and multistepped. I watch it unfold for one bird. One of the animal keepers, Debbie Sears, with a net in one hand, opens the door to the enclosure. The condors respond well to very slow movements. These condors are wild. The zoo attempts to keep them as unfamiliar with humans as possible. I stand in the doorway, watching silently as Debbie walks slowly over to one of the large birds, which is watching her. It attempts to fly as she tries to place the net over it. After two tries she is able to slip the net over its head. She makes sure that the entire bird is covered. She then holds it firmly by its tail feathers and lifts it into her arms, one hand covering its face, the other supporting its body.

Another animal keeper, Jenny Schmidt, moves quickly to get everything in place for treatment. As Debbie holds the condor, Jenny injects it with a substance (calcium edetate) that will remove the lead from its body. After the injection, she will hook a saline IV to the bird to help keep its kidneys healthy. Within the hour, the condor is finished with the treatment and given a blood test to monitor its lead level.

Condors are carefully captured for treatments at the zoo. Keeping wild condors healthy has become a large part of the animal keepers' jobs.

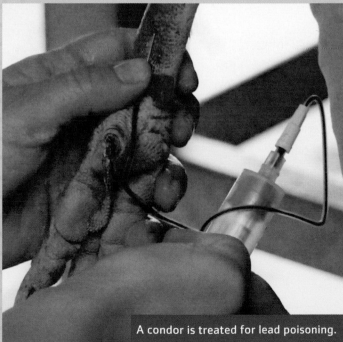

A condor is treated for lead poisoning.

This full container demonstrates the amount of chelation treatments the animal keepers have had to conduct to treat lead-poisoned condors.

FATHER/DAUGHTER CONDOR VOLUNTEERS

Not all the people who monitor condors are scientists. David Cortes and his daughter, thirteen-year-old Alicia, volunteer to monitor the condors living in the Los Padres National Forest. Like the scientists who monitor the condor population, they love helping wildlife and they know a lot about condors.

"You have to know what a healthy condor looks like to be able to identify its age and tell if it is sick," says Alicia. "You also have to know how to identify crop sizes and what that means. If you can't see the crop, then the condor probably hasn't eaten for a while. If it is big, then you know it ate recently."

Alicia and her dad have spent many hours watching the condors. "Condors are beautifully ugly animals," claims Alicia. Sometimes as Alicia and her dad are watching, a condor makes eye contact with them. That's a very special moment that not many people have had.

"Being out there in the wild, watching those magnificent birds that are living oblivious to what is going on a few miles away in one of the busiest cities, and feeling part of something bigger than yourself is powerful," says David. What a wonderful feeling to know that with their help this great bird is able to soar again.

MORE TOXINS HAMPER RECOVERY

A report in 2016 showed that, in addition to lead, there is large amount of toxic chemicals—some of which are a result of pesticides—in the fatty marine animal carcasses that condors are eating. Thus the pesticides used on land are not only having an impact on the insects they target, they are also seeping into the water and poisoning fish along with any creature that eats the fish. Scientists have also found higher levels of mercury and pesticides in the condors that feed on dead marine mammals. These harmful levels might further hamper condor recovery efforts.

It is interesting to note that condors, having been on this earth for more than a million years, have outlived such early peers of the ancient Pleistocene period as the giant beavers, sloths, and other megafauna that perished in a mass-extinction event. Condors survived mostly because they were able to forage on marine life, whereas their peers could not. Today, feeding on marine life could end up being their downfall.

Yet, even though there are still challenges to face, the California condor recovery program has achieved wonderful successes.

MILESTONES!

Time to celebrate! A female condor chick hatched, survived, and fledged from a nest at Pinnacles National Park in 2016! This is big news. No chick has accomplished all those things here since the 1890s. Others have been born in the wild at Pinnacles, but none has survived long enough to fledge

This young condor still has its dark plumage. Condors don't show their iconic coloration until they reach six to eight years old.

from the nest. This is great news for the recovery program. Hurrah for condor chick #828!

Seeing a wild condor is an exhilarating experience. Imagine how it feels to reintroduce to the wild a bird that has been in captivity for thirty years.

Dr. Peter Bloom had that very experience. He was one of the original biologists who captured AC4 in 1987, and he was on hand to set him free on December 29, 2015.

AC4, with an orange tag that reads #20, flies free now. He is one of four remaining condors of the original twenty-two that were taken into captivity. While in captivity, he sired thirty chicks that were released into the wild. Now he joins them in the skies!

"Watching this California condor, who has been so instrumental to the recovery of his species, rejoin the wild flock, is an emotional and historic moment," said Joseph Brandt, lead condor biologist with the Fish and Wildlife Service. "It's like seeing him come full circle."

Thinking back to Janet Hamber's words in her field journal, where she wrote of her sadness, anger, and hope for the future of these ancient birds, makes me so very thankful that we have scientists who work tirelessly, with such dedication, and are willing to take risks for these fragile populations.

CAPTIVE BREEDING SUCCESS

Just like California condors, black-footed ferrets have been brought back from the brink of extinction through a similar captive breeding/reintroduction recovery plan. There were only ten black-footed ferrets known to be in the wild in 1985. As with the condors, these few animals were taken into captivity in 1987 for a chance at a recovery program.

Fortunately, this species was able to be reintroduced into the wild and is also an Endangered Species Act success story, but not all captive breeding programs are so successful. If legislators and scientists are not able to correct the issues that brought a species to the brink in the first place, the newly released individuals won't be able to survive. Every species needs a livable, clean, safe habitat above all.

When swimming, alligators are watertight and can stay underwater at rest for about two hours. If it is very cold, they can stay under for up to eight hours.

AMERICAN ALLIGATORS SWIM IN THE SOUTH

A PLACE IN THE WILD

I'm in the Everglades in South Florida during the dry season. For some of the country, the winter brings snow and ice, but for the Everglades the season is dry and filled with the sound of birds courting and nesting among the sawgrass and hardwood hammocks.

The Everglades is a unique spot, the only one like it in the world. The naturalist Marjory Stoneman Douglas named it the "river of grass." Like a river, it has water, but it also has a species of grass called sawgrass that moves in the wind the way a river ripples. It is the home of many different species, including the American alligator (*Alligator mississippiensis*).

Alligators, members of the crocodilian family of reptiles, have been on our planet for about 200 million years. They inhabit much of the southern United States, from Texas to the Carolinas. Like their croc relatives, they play a crucial role in the environment. As top predators, they contribute to the health of their home by preying on rodents and other creatures that might overrun the wetland vegetation.

The Everglades, known as the "river of grass," is one of the homes of the American alligator.

Alligator claws may look dangerous, but they are actually used for digging, not for slashing prey.

But that isn't all alligators do to help their marshy landscape. They create holes by "using their faces as shovels and their tails as plows," and these holes stay full of water in the wet season and even hold water after the rains stop. The water helps alligators regulate their body temperature. Being cold-blooded reptiles, gators stay under the water on cold days to stay warm and on hot days to stay cool.

Wildlife has gathered at the hole in front of me. Storks stand in the grass. A turtle sits on a small branch. And the large black gators lie on the banks, basking in the hot sun to warm their bodies and help them digest. Some females are accompanied by their young. Others lie beside male gators.

These holes, the size of backyard swimming pools, create an essential living space for many other animals, including turtles, birds, and fish. But as my park ranger explains it, the "gators invite all of them over for a pool party and then enjoy the good eats."

ALLIGATOR HOLE ECOLOGY

Alligator holes function as a way to increase the diversity of the Everglades and other areas where they exist. During the dry season, rangers have measured more than twenty fish per cubic foot in a gator hole. These concentrations of fish help nesting birds feed their young. In 1968 the conservationist Frank Craighead defined alligator holes as having these three traits:

1. A depression in the muck or limestone bedrock

2. Water to fill the resulting basin

3. Alligators to create and maintain the hole

American alligators create holes that draw wildlife—and a nice meal!

HUNTED TO THE BRINK

"The alligator dominated the freshwater marshes of South Florida much as did the buffalo on the Great Plains before white man appeared," wrote the wildlife scientist Frank C. Craighead in 1968.

Alligators seem to be everywhere these days, but things were once very different. American alligators were threatened with extinction by hunters who killed them for food and for the production of fancy alligator-skin shoes, handbags, and boots.

But it wasn't the rich and famous who began sporting alligator skins; early Civil War Confederate soldiers wore alligator boots and sat atop alligator saddles. The skins were durable, and the abundance of the reptiles made these goods economical.

After that war, manufacturers in New York and New Jersey began purchasing Louisiana alligator skins to make boots, shoes, and purses, and other companies bought alligator oil for use in machinery.

"Three persons residing in the parish of Assumption, last year killed 9,000 alligators, saved the oil and sold the hides," the Lafayette *Advertiser* reported on June 3, 1882. "The price of the hides is 75 cents apiece."

In 1905, the same newspaper warned of an unexpected consequence of hunting the gators. According to the paper, alligators helped guard against flooding by eating muskrats that dug holes in the levees.

The Louisiana Department of Wildlife and Fisheries estimates that from

Female alligators will often stay together.

1880 to 1933, approximately 3.5 million Louisiana alligators were killed for their skins—an average of 64,815 per year.

And alligators were also hunted in most southern states, including Florida. As Marjory Stoneman Douglas wrote in *The Everglades: River of Grass,* "One of the Lopez boys would later take ten thousand alligators in one month of night fire-hunting from a lake near Shark River and sell the skins for fifty cents apiece."

A SPECIES SAVED

With all this hunting, the American alligator earned its right to be one of the first animals listed on the Endangered Species List. In 1962, even before the list was formed, commercial and recreational hunting of the species was prohibited. But that wasn't enough. The American alligator needed extra measures, which the list provided. It needed a recovery plan.

The U.S. Fish and Wildlife Service plan for recovery included captive breeding on alligator farms and reintroduction into the wild. Alligator monitoring programs were established. The reptile recovered pretty quickly for a species that had suffered such a serious population loss. Part of this was because of their breeding patterns. Female alligators lay between thirty and ninety eggs in a muddy nest each spring. The nest, covered with decomposing vegetation, supplies heat to incubate the eggs for sixty-five days. The embryos will develop to be male or female depending on how hot the nest is. If the temperature is in the low eighties (in degrees Fahrenheit), the baby alligators will be female. If it rises to the nineties, they will be male.

OFF THE LIST

The American alligator was delisted as endangered in 1987 but remains listed as threatened to help protect the threatened American crocodile (*Crocodylus acutus*), which looks very similar. Crocs have a narrower snout than gators have. They do, however, share some of the same habitat

Can the Everglades support two top predators—the native American alligator and the invasive Burmese python?

in Florida. Yet even though the gator population has recovered and monitored hunting is now allowed, we do not have the privilege of resting on our laurels. Alligators and their habitat are under attack.

Unseen by me in the Everglades are countless invasive animal species, such as tegu lizards and Burmese pythons, that are wreaking havoc on this diverse ecosystem and the alligator population. In fact, wildlife biologist Joe Wasilewski was dealing with the removal of pythons every day of my visit. "We're tired of studying these invasive species—now we have to do something about them," he says.

The omnivorous Argentine black and white tegu (*Salvator merianae*), gold tegu (*Tupinambis teguixin*), and red tegu (*Tupinambis rufescens*) lizards that have invaded Florida will eat everything, especially eggs—any eggs. The four-foot (1.2 meter) lizards have powerful jaws and eat any eggs they find, including those of alligators and sea turtles. Tegus can swim, crawl, or climb to reach their next meal, making them a big threat to native wildlife. One trapper in South Florida, using live traps that don't kill the

You can see the pointed difference in these two skulls. Alligators have a more rounded skull than crocodiles.

captured animal, caught eight hundred tegus in a period of only two and a half years. Many of his trapped lizards are shipped to Asia, where they are kept as pets. Still more await capture.

Burmese pythons are just as destructive. They are purchased in pet shops when they are tiny and can be easily kept in a tank and fed crickets and baby mice. However, as the python matures, it grows very large. Soon it requires adult mice, then rats, then chickens. Many are set free in the Everglades at this point, but some are kept longer, needing even larger food. Imagine what they can eat as they mature in the Everglades—pretty much anything they want, including endangered Florida panthers and alligators.

There are many feral pythons in the Everglades now, and they lay upwards of a hundred eggs at a time, multiplying their population exponentially. Sadly, Burmese pythons are threatened in their native range in Southeast Asia.

Fortunately, there are not only professionals working to eradicate these species, but also hobbyists who know the area and hunt them for hours on end. They can find lizards and snakes from all over the world in one night—pythons, iguanas, chameleons, and tegus. Permits are issued to enable data to be collected and to make sure that local natural species are not killed by mistake.

"Between the pythons and tegus, it's devastating to the native fauna of the Everglades," says Joe, who has seen tegus eating through a nest of alligator eggs.

MORE THREATS

The American alligator population also faces other challenges today, including climate change. As temperatures rise, greater numbers of male alligators will hatch. This may significantly change the alligator population. In addition, their brackish freshwater marsh habitat may face an increase of salt water as sea levels rise.

Another recent concern is the health of the alligators in the Everglades. Scientists have reported that many gators have been found to weigh 80 percent of what they should weigh, are reproducing less, and, sadly, are

Newly hatched gators live in groups with their mother called *pods.* They will stay under the protection of their mother for a few years.

perishing at younger ages, warranting more studies to find out why this is happening.

We've seen that we cannot take strong gator population numbers for granted. These are all reasons to keep monitoring and protecting these reptiles.

WHAT TO DO IF YOU SEE A TEGU

Take a photo.

Record the location.

Report the sighting by phone or online: 1-888-IVE-GOT1 or ivegot1.org.

You can also download an app: IveGot1 reporting app.

Other ways to help: Don't let an exotic pet loose! If you can't keep a pet, surrender it at an Exotic Pet Amnesty Day event in Florida or call the hotline for information at 1-888-IVE-GOT1.

There are roughly 50,000 gators in the Everglades today.

IN THE GLADES

I'm standing on a wooden platform on the Anhinga Trail in Everglades National Park. The sun is beginning to set, and the alligators in front of me are starting to move from their basking spots. They've spent the day soaking up the rays and will be hunting when the sun goes down. One swims away from me into the sawgrass-lined water. I watch, in the golden light, until the tail's graceful curve is out of sight.

AMERICAN BISON: GIVE ME A HOME WHERE THE BUFFALO ROAM . . .

HOME ON THE RANGE

It's a beautiful spring day in New York State's Hudson Valley, and the residents, both animal and human, shake off the long winter. Just over the fence from me, in the warm afternoon sunshine, is Gem Farms' herd of shaggy American bison (*Bison bison*). These animals, also known as buffalo, are huge. They can weigh between 900 and 2,000 pounds (between 408.2 kg and 907.2 kg), and they reach a height of 6 to 6.5 feet. They can run at 30 miles per hour (48.3 km per hour) and leap up to 6 feet (1.8 m) in the air. I can feel their power as they move, and the ground rumbles gently beneath my feet at this close distance.

More than two hundred years ago there were wild buffalo roaming free east of the Mississippi, but not anymore. Imagine the surprise, then, when a herd of twenty-two American bison broke free from this very farm in upstate New York and swam across the Hudson River into the state's capital city, Albany. It was a scene straight out of the Wild West as they stampeded across a highway and invaded a residential area.

This buffalo is part of a herd in the Hudson Valley of New York State, where buffalo have not ranged in the wild for over two hundred years.

Tragically, the animals that broke through their fence that year were too large and dangerous to herd into a truck, and they were killed before they hurt anyone during their stampede. American bison don't have an *off* switch; they just keep running. Wranglers joke about them, saying that you can herd a buffalo anywhere *he* wants to go. That these escaped animals were not wild but were being raised for food didn't make their loss any less unfortunate.

As I watch the herd in front of me munch on hay, my tiny, normally quiet dog barks a warning from my car. His yipping doesn't faze these behemoths one bit. He's about the size of one hoof. "You're right, Boo, these animals are huge," I say, confirming his concern. He settles down as soon as I'm back within the safety of the car.

FREE RANGE

There are only about fifty buffalo behind the wire fence in front of me, nowhere near the estimated 20 to 30 million that once thundered across North America. But even so, they are impressive. *The Journals of Lewis and Clark* describe western herds "so numerous" that they "darkened the whole plains." How could such a huge population of these great wild mammals have dwindled to only *thirty-nine* by the year 1900?

Disease and loss of habitat were contributing factors, but the main cause was overhunting on a grand scale. When buffalo were plentiful, Native

Bison eat about 24 pounds (11 kg) of vegetation per day. On the prairie they foraged for native grasses and kicked up the soil as they moved and ate, enabling prairie plants and animals to flourish.

Americans harvested about 2 million of them a year from wild herds. Every part of the animal was put to use: moccasins, blankets, cradles, leggings, beds, belts, tepee covers, and other items were made from buffalo hides. The hair was used for rope, moccasin lining, doll stuffing, horse halters, pillow filler, and more. The meat was eaten immediately after the hunt or made into jerky or dried into strips to eat later.

For the tribes of the Great Plains, the buffalo was their entire universe. Their culture was intimately connected with North America's great mammal, both physically and spiritually.

LOOK TO THE MOVIES

Watch the buffalo hunt scene in the Academy Award–winning movie *Dances with Wolves* and you can get a feel for what a Sioux hunt was like when the buffalo, known to them as *tatanka,* ran free across the plains. If you watch the entire well-researched movie, you will have some insight into what life was like when settlers and the United States government moved into the territory.

THE GREAT SLAUGHTER

Early American farmers and ranchers killed buffalos to create room for their livestock to graze. That made a dent in the buffalo population, but only a small one. Then the U.S. Army, under the direction of General William Tecumseh Sherman, went to war with the Native American tribes of the plains. Bitter United States soldiers struck out against their Native American enemies by killing buffalo, the main source of food, shelter, and clothing for more than twenty-four tribes. Sherman even convinced President Grant to veto a bill that would have protected the buffalo from commercial hunting. War was raging, and buffalo were caught in the middle.

If that wasn't enough, railroads crisscrossing the land divided the herds and, at the same time, brought more people, more hunters, to their grazing lands. Some train passengers shot buffalo for sport from their open train windows, leaving the rotting corpses to waste on the plains.

HOW FAST THEY FELL

"A solitary hunter equipped with an accurate large-bore Sharps rifle could fell up to 100 buffalo in a single stand, and this technology marked the beginning of a plains-wide slaughter that within four decades would reduce an estimated 30 million animals to less than 1,000. It was the greatest mass destruction of warm-blooded animals in human history, far worse than what the world's whaling fleets had already accomplished, and as Sitting Bull was to lament years later, 'A cold wind blew across the prairie when the last buffalo fell. A death wind for my people.'" —from *The Heart of Everything That Is: The Untold Story of Red Cloud* by Bob Drury and Tom Clavin

Historic image of a Native American buffalo hunt.

In fact, the famous entertainer William Frederick Cody, who became known as Buffalo Bill, received his nickname after he honored a contract to supply the Kansas Pacific Railroad workers with buffalo meat. He killed 4,282 American bison in a period of eighteen months.

The years between 1820 and 1880 became known as the Great Slaughter. The bison population had decreased so much by 1889 that, as the conservationist William T. Hornaday wrote, a bison's death was "now such an event that it is immediately chronicled by the Associated Press and telegraphed all over the country."

WITHIN THE ECOSYSTEM

Nobody understood that the survival of the buffalo was intermingled with the survival of the Great Plains itself, not just of its Native people. The buffalo were part of a complex ecosystem. Native people traditionally set fires in the plains. The buffalo, attracted to the fresh grasses that grew in the burned areas, maintained the prairie ecosystem by limiting tree growth in two ways: by grazing and by rubbing their horns on the bark of saplings.

There are fewer than 5,000 American bison in the wild today.

ONE MAN'S MISSION

William T. Hornaday, charged in the 1880s with collecting specimens for the Smithsonian, discovered the devastatingly low numbers of wild bison. He was shocked at how quickly the population had been destroyed, and he feared that he was too late to save these iconic mammals. Unlike most people at that time, who didn't recognize the loss, Hornaday did, and he had the perseverance and tenacity to make a difference.

"There is no reason to hope that a single wild and unprotected individual [buffalo] will remain alive in ten years hence," Hornaday wrote at the conclusion of his book *The Extermination of the American Bison*, dated May 1, 1889.

A stack of bison skulls piled up taller than a man were to be used for fertilizer in the 1890s.

Fortunately, others were also watching the buffalo disappear from the plains. James McKay, Charles Alloway, Charles Goodnight, Walking Coyote, Frederic Dupree, and Charles "Buffalo" Jones all began capturing the last remaining wild bison in the 1870s, creating their own private herds.

In 1905 Hornaday founded the American Bison Society with President Theodore Roosevelt and others to try to prevent the bison's extinction. At that time, there were only a few hundred buffalo remaining in the wild.

THE ROAD TO RECOVERY

In 1901, when only twenty-four bison remained wild in the United States and the only others were living in Yellowstone or in private herds, Congress allocated $15,000 to purchase twenty-one bison from private owners to add to the Yellowstone herd. For the first half of the twentieth century these bison were kept in captivity at the Lamar Buffalo Ranch in Wyoming's Lamar Valley. After the herd grew to an acceptable size, they were released into Yellowstone to breed with the park's wild bison. They were also used to add to the herds on other public and tribal lands.

NEVER MAKING THE LIST

Even though the American bison population fell to a dangerously low number, they were never placed on the Endangered Species List. A related subspecies, the wood bison, was classified as endangered in 1979 and downlisted to threatened in 1988. American bison were placed on the Red List, classified as near threatened.

THE AMERICAN BISON SOCIETY

William Hornaday would be pleased to see that the organization he helped found is still going strong and celebrating its many accomplishments. In 2016 it released a "report card" that showed what could be achieved when conservationists, government agencies, tribes, and the public come together for a common cause. In this case, entities from Mexico, Canada, and the United States made the impossible attainable.

Not only did the team help bring about the passage of the National Bison Legacy Act, it also contributed to the reintroduction of the historic Pablo-Allard bison to their ancestral home on the Blackfeet Indian Reservation in Montana. The original Montana herd, owned by Michel Pablo, was sold and shipped to Canada between 1901 and 1912, after the United States declined the sale. William Hornaday would be jumping for joy!

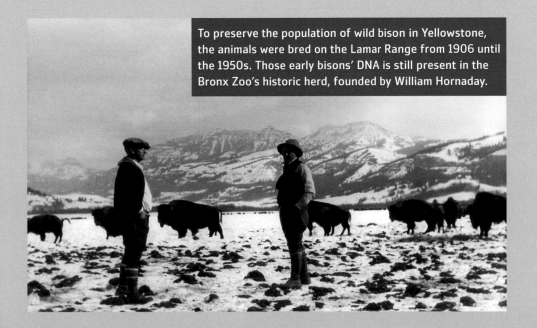

To preserve the population of wild bison in Yellowstone, the animals were bred on the Lamar Range from 1906 until the 1950s. Those early bisons' DNA is still present in the Bronx Zoo's historic herd, founded by William Hornaday.

SUPER-BEEF

The Yellowstone National Park herds are genetically 100 percent American bison; however, most of the bison that graze on private lands today have been bred with cattle. Early cattle ranchers who owned bison in the late nineteenth and twentieth centuries bred these creatures together, hoping to create a super-beef animal. Privatization of the bison population has prevented the species from becoming extinct, but most now have some cattle genes, and they are not genetically the same as the free-range herds in Yellowstone.

"When people went looking for bison later, they had to go to the private cattlemen who owned them, and in many cases those private guys were producing hybrids in a failed attempt to develop hardier beef cat-

The majority of bison alive today live on farms; farms across the country sell bison meat. There are fewer than 5,000 in the wild.

tle," says Dr. James Derr, a Texas A&M University professor of veterinary pathobiology.

Of the estimated five hundred thousand buffalo in North America today, only three genetically pure herds exist: one in Yellowstone, one in Wind Cave National Park in South Dakota, and a newer herd of about 350 buffalo in Utah's Henry Mountains.

CELEBRATE NATIONAL BISON DAY!

In 2016 the American bison was declared the national mammal of the United States. This historic designation is meant not only to prevent the bison from going extinct but also to recognize its ecological, cultural, historical, and economic importance to the country. The bison joins the eagle, the oak tree, and the rose as national symbols of America.

Celebrate National Bison Day on November 5!

The buffalo nickel was designed by James Earle Fraser and was produced by the U.S. Mint from 1913 to 1938.

BACK IN BANFF

Buffalo were reintroduced to the eastern slopes of Canada's Banff National Park in 2017. This began a five-year reintroduction program. Celebrated by First Nations communities and conservationists, sixteen animals—ten pregnant heifers and six young bulls—were brought to Banff from Elk Island National Park. By the time Banff National Park was created in 1887, the native bison had already been killed off. The call to reintroduce the animals came in 2010, after the International Union for Conservation of Nature (IUCN) released a report on the ecology and history of bison in North America. It is another example of how this international body can influence and encourage recovery programs throughout the world. It will be interesting to watch as this new herd grows and makes Banff its home.

The American bison is now our national mammal, thanks to unanimous bipartisan legislation, proclaimed as such by President Barack Obama

THE REVERED BISON

As a cultural touchstone for Native Americans, bison are revered. The Inter Tribal Bison Council (ITBC) was formed in 1990 to support the reestablishment of bison herds on Native tribal lands. It has a membership of fifty-six tribes in nineteen states and a collective herd of more than fifteen thousand bison. The ITBC works to coordinate education programs and the transfer of surplus bison from national parks to tribal lands.

when he signed the National Bison Legacy Act into law in 2016. Supporters of the act came from all walks of life and all parts of the country. For some, the bison represented western culture. For others it honored Native American tribes. Still more celebrated the unique partnership of ranchers, politicians, conservationists, and Native Americans that helped restore the population. All see the bison as a uniquely American mammal.

THE STORY CONTINUES

Bison continue to draw tourists to national parks, zoos, and wildlife reserves throughout the United States. They are a keystone species, meaning that other species depend on them for survival—in this case it is the prairie environment that needs them. They also help drive the economy. Yet, although they have been brought back from the brink of extinction, they still face an uncertain future outside the boundaries of our national parks.

Ranchers fear a disease called brucellosis, which they claim is carried by the bison and can infect elk and cattle. The disease can cause pregnant bison heifers to lose their calves. The bacterium associated with brucellosis is not native to the bison. It was brought by domestic cattle to the bison population as early as 1917. Today, about half of Yellowstone's herd tests positive for brucellosis, although there has not been a single case of transference from bison to cattle.

The park's bison herd numbered fifty-five hundred animals in 2016, which is five hundred more than the park deems sustainable. The population is maintained using two methods—legal hunts outside the park and capturing bison near the boundary to transfer to nearby Native American tribes for slaughter. Wildlife activists don't agree with either of these approaches. In 2016 they sued the federal government, requesting that the Yellowstone buffalo be listed once more as threatened or endangered in order to protect them from hunting.

Roughly 4 million visitors come to Yellowstone each year, most to see the wild bison, one of America's great restoration success stories. What will the future hold for these iconic animals? Will our national mammal roam within the confines of Yellowstone, on tribal lands, or behind farm

MASS BISON SLAUGHTER

On February 2, 2017, as I finished writing this chapter, a deal was disclosed between the U.S. Department of Agriculture, the state of Montana, and Yellowstone National Park that would allow the slaughter of up to 1,300 of Yellowstone's 5,500 wild bison that migrate from that national park into Montana—sparing only 25 to be given to Native tribes to start their own herds. The support for this deal comes from ranchers concerned about the transmission of brucellosis from bison to domestic livestock, although there have not been any transmissions recorded. As we see with many of these species, sometimes we take a few steps forward only to take a step backwards.

fences, only to end up on our grocery store shelves? There are dedicated conservationists who are determined not to let that happen. Such organizations as The Nature Conservancy in Indiana are striving to restore prairie habitat. In 2016, twenty-three bison were released on the prairie in Indiana's Kankakee Sands. And the American Bison Society is still hard at work making sure bison have a future in the United States.

What a gift it is to have bison still with us!

Join the Buffalo Field Campaign in protecting free-roaming wild buffalo herds and urge Congress to list wild bison under the Endangered Species Act. buffalofieldcampaign.org

NATIONAL
WILDLIFE
REFUGE

UNAUTHORIZED ENTRY
PROHIBITED

U.S. DEPARTMENT OF THE INTERIOR
FISH AND WILDLIFE SERVICE

CALL TO ACTION!

GOOD NEWS

A volunteer fire department formed in 1736 became known as Benjamin Franklin's Bucket Brigade. Members were required to arrive at every fire with six leather buckets that they would fill with water and pass to one another in a long line to help extinguish the flames. Each firefighter was essential in combating the fire. If even one was missing, the brigade would suffer.

When I interviewed Dr. Cary Fowler for *The Story of Seeds,* he told me that his work in helping to save our global crops was just his way of being a part of the "bucket brigade." Like Dr. Fowler, the scientists, volunteers, legislators, and conservationists dedicated to saving species from the brink of extinction are all part of the "bucket brigade."

With their help I have been able to hear about many wonderful "firsts" as I finish up this book. As we all know, "firsts" are much better to note than "lasts" in the struggle to conserve endangered species.

In April of 2016, the first whooping crane chick was born in the wild in Louisiana, making it the first crane hatched in the state since 1939.

For the first time in a hundred years, a wood bison—a subspecies of the American bison and the largest land mammal in North America—was born in the wilds of Alaska.

Just after I was in California to study the condors, a condor chick was fledged at nearby Pinnacles National Park—the first there since 1890!

There was also good news for other endangered species, such as black-footed ferrets. Once believed to be extinct, they have been reintroduced to the ranch where they were rediscovered thirty-five years ago.

Conservation scientists in Puerto Rico have been celebrating the recovery of one of the world's rarest and most critically endangered birds, the Puerto Rican parrot. Not only are they breeding the birds successfully at an aviary, but, even better, wild pairs are nesting in the wild without the help of nesting boxes.

And the giant panda has been downgraded from endangered to vulnerable on the IUCN Red List of Threatened Species.

These success stories give us reason to celebrate and remind us that together we can make a difference. All of our efforts are important.

THE STATE OF THE LIST

Unfortunately, there still remain close to 500 endangered animals on America's Endangered Species List. Out of 410 wild mammal species in this country, more than 80 are on the list. This number is astronomical. Clearly there is more work to be done.

For some species, such as the dusky seaside sparrow, the ESA designation came too late to help it recover. But we have been pretty fortunate. Of the fifteen hundred species that have been listed and protected under the ESA, roughly ten have gone extinct. For most others, like the California condor, the protection of the list was just the lifeline they needed.

PLANT NATIVE PLANTS

Amid the roar of flying airplanes, it is difficult to think of butterflies calling the Los Angeles International Airport home. But in fact, tucked into the buckwheat shrubs near the end of the runways are the chrysalises of the tiny endangered El Segundo blue butterfly, just waiting to take flight.

How on earth can a butterfly, seemingly so fragile, survive habitat destruction, drought, traffic, noise, and all the other things that come with a modern airport?

This tiny blue butterfly is like many other creatures—it depends on one kind of food. In this case, coast buckwheat. Although the butterfly has dwindled in numbers, scientists, knowing that it relied on the buckwheat, planted it in large numbers and pulled out the nonnative plants that competed with it. The population began to increase, and there are now an estimated 125,000 of these creatures taking flight each summer.

What Can You Do? Find out what native plants you can plant in your area that will help wildlife.

ENDANGERED SPECIES ACT FACES CHALLENGES

Although the Endangered Species Act has saved countless species from extinction for more than forty years, it continues to face unrelenting scrutiny and attacks.

Continuous pressure from many commercial interests has put this important environmental legislation in jeopardy. In addition, ESA protection can be withdrawn without eliminating the problems that led to a species' population decrease in the first place, such as large-scale habitat destruction and climate change. For example, listing polar bears as endangered cannot force an international agreement on greenhouse-gas emissions to combat the climate change that threatens their survival.

As climate change puts even more wildlife at risk, it is imperative that we keep this legislation strong so that our grandchildren and great-grandchildren can enjoy all Earth's creatures and the places they call home.

In addition, we need to keep our focus on habitats and native plants. We might be able to save many species, but if we don't save their homes, they can live only in zoos. Is that the world we want to live in? For all the effort and expense that it takes to restore a species, it would be so much easier if we could prevent wildlife populations from reaching that critical state in the first place.

Each time I am fortunate enough to conduct my research in the wild, a little piece of it lands in my heart. I am hoping that in reading about these species, you will also take a piece with you. In that way we will all be joined in the "bucket brigade" to protect our planet and we can strive to make a difference wherever we live. There are so many ways for you to get involved. Perhaps one of the stories in this book might just inspire you to act.

TAKE THE LEAD OUT

Become an advocate for wildlife. California condors are not the only species to suffer from lead poisoning. As long as lead ammunition is used in the United States, we will have lead in our environment, our wildlife, and our own bodies. You can help to inform hunters in your area that lead ammunition kills more than once. Let them know that non-lead bullets stay in one piece after impact. This means that, unlike lead bullets, they can be cleanly removed without leaving fragments behind. They will not only keep condors, eagles, and other animals healthy, they will also keep hunters and their families healthy. *What Can You Do?* Contact your representatives and ask them to act on behalf of wildlife and our health and ban lead ammunition.

PARROT SUCCESS

Conservation scientists in Puerto Rico have been celebrating the recovery of one of the world's rarest and most critically endangered birds, the Puerto Rican parrot. In 1990, only a handful of these green parrots lived in the wild; today about one hundred are thriving. Ricardo Valentin, an aviculturist—a person who cares for and breeds birds—with the Puerto Rico Department of Natural and Environmental Resources, describes the successful breeding program as facing an "egg tsunami" at the José L. Vivaldi Memorial Aviary. Not only are they breeding the birds successfully at the aviary, but, even better, wild pairs are nesting in the wild without the help of nesting boxes.

KEEP MICROTRASH IN THE TRASH

Easy-peasy! Don't throw bottle caps and other small items on the ground! We've controlled littering for the most part; now let's wipe out the careless tossing of microtrash wherever we live, so that it doesn't find its way into the mouths of wildlife. *What Can You Do?* Begin an anti-litter campaign in your school or neighborhood!

GIVE A WHOOP

Preserving wetlands helps not only whooping cranes but also countless other species, and even our water supply. Learn about the wetlands in your area and help protect them.

What Can You Do? Pick up litter and keep storm drains clean. Buy notebooks with unbleached paper. The bleaching process contains toxic chemicals that often contaminate water. Always reduce, reuse, and recycle!

LIMIT THE USE OF PESTICIDES

Millions of birds continue to die each year from the use of pesticides on U.S. farms. Limiting our use will keep our birds—and us—healthier. *What Can You Do?* Shop organic!

SHARE THE LOVE FOR WILDLIFE

Help spread the word about your favorite species. *What Can You Do?* Write a letter to your local paper. Make a classroom display. Form your own wolf pack in order to share the importance of wolves or another species with your family, scout troop, classmates, and friends.

BECOME A CONDOR SPOTTER

You and your family can volunteer to become condor spotters if you live in California. *What Can You Do?* Contact your local Audubon Society or the Santa Barbara Zoo to volunteer.

These are just a fraction of the actions we can take to keep our planet healthy. Humans have the ability to bring wildlife to the brink of extinction, but we also have the ability to fight on its behalf. Everyone can make a difference.

Keeping our earth diverse will keep it strong for all its living organisms, including us!

LEARN MORE

WATCH

Buffalo Hunt, scene from *Dances with Wolves.* www.youtube.com/watch?v=dPze
   Y9itfLE.

Never Cry Wolf, Walt Disney, 1983, based on Farley Mowat's book of the same title.

Anna, Emma and the Condors. KRBC Public Media, Natural Heroes series, 2011.
   naturalheroes.org/videos/anna-emma-and-the-condors/.

Jim Brandenburg's project Nature 365 has videos of eagles, bison, wolves, and more:
   nature365.tv/presentation-du-projet/.

First Crane Hatchlings. www.youtube.com/watch?v=lBXEonuwSOI.

Fly Away Home. Sony Pictures Home Entertainment, August 7, 2001.

See the capture and release of condor AC4 at www.flickr.com/photos/usfws_pacificsw
   /23462645594/in/album-72157662526009495/.

Wolf Conservation Center Webcam. nywolf.org/webcams.

Take a peek into a condor nest and perhaps you'll even see a chick fledge!
   www.facebook.com/TheCondorCave.

Take a look at the Savannah Wildlife Refuge: www.youtube.com/watch?v=N6Q5MN
   dPKGo.

Exotic Invaders: Pythons in the Everglades. Explica Media, 2015. Available on Netflix.

Check out WCC's PACK members Henry and Jonah's website about wolves: rwrf.weebly
   .com.

READ

Endangered Species Act Conference Report. www.eswr.com/docs/lh/426-488.pdf.

Jean Craighead George, *Galapagos George.* HarperCollins, 2014.

Kitson Jazynka, *Mission: Wolf Rescue.* National Geographic Kids, 2014.

Farley Mowat, *Never Cry Wolf.* Bantam Books, 1973.

Dorothy Hinshaw Patent, *The Buffalo and the Indians.* Clarion, 2006

Stephen Swinburne, *Once a Wolf: How Wildlife Biologists Fought to Bring Back the Gray Wolf.* Houghton Mifflin, 2001.

Examine the numbers of bald eagle nesting pairs recorded by state from 1990 to 2006 by the U.S. Fish and Wildlife Service: www.fws.gov/midwest/eagle/population/nos_state_tbl.html.

Read the *Citizens' Guide to the Endangered Species Act*: earthjustice.org/sites/default/files/library/reports/Citizens_Guide_ESA.pdf.

ORGANIZATIONS

The Peregrine Fund works on behalf of raptors, including California condors, eagles, falcons, and more: peregrinefund.org.

Adopt an eagle online from the Audubon Society: store.audubon.org/bird/bald-eagle.

International Crane Foundation: www.savingcranes.org.

Wolf Conservation Center: nywolf.org.

For info on lead-free ammunition: huntingwithnonlead.org.

Aldo Leopold Foundation, Baraboo, Wisconsin. Visit to see Leopold's shack for yourself or take a video journey online: www.aldoleopold.org.

GO

WHOOPING CRANES:

Whooping Crane Festival, Aransas National Wildlife Refuge, Texas: www.whooping
cranefestival.org/.

International Crane Foundation, Baraboo, Wisconsin: www.savingcranes.org.

WOLVES:

Wolf Howl—Algonquin Provincial Park, Ontario, Canada: www.algonquinpark.on.ca
/visit/programs/wolf-howls.php.

Wolf Connection, Acton, California: wolfconnection.org.

Wolf Conservation Center, South Salem, New York: nywolf.org.

EAGLES:

Share your bald eagle sightings at www.baldeagleinfo.com/eagle/eagle1.html.

The Klamath Basin Refuges, Tulelake, California

Iroquois National Wildlife Refuge, Basom, New York

Mason Neck National Wildlife Refuge, Woodbridge, Virginia

Patuxent Research Refuge, Laurel, Maryland

Sherburne National Wildlife Refuge, Zimmerman, Minnesota

Squaw Creek National Wildlife Refuge, Mound City, Missouri

DeSoto National Wildlife Refuge, Missouri Valley, Iowa

Chassahowitzka National Wildlife Refuge, Crystal River, Florida

Ridgefield National Wildlife Refuge, Ridgefield, Washington

Reelfoot National Wildlife Refuge, Union City, Tennessee

North Platte National Wildlife Refuge, Scottsbluff, Nebraska

Kenai National Wildlife Refuge, Soldotna, Alaska

GALÁPAGOS TORTOISES:

Galapagos—How Tourists Can Help: www.galapagos.org

CALIFORNIA CONDORS:

Santa Barbara Zoo: www.sbzoo.org.

Los Padres National Forest, California

Grand Canyon National Park, Arizona

AMERICAN ALLIGATORS:

Everglades National Park, Florida

Savannah Wildlife Refuge, Georgia

Rockefeller Refuge, Lake Charles, Louisiana

American alligators can also be found at many other locations throughout the southern
    United States.

AMERICAN BISON:

Farewell Lake Bison Herd, Alaska

Delta Junction Bison Range, Alaska

Yellowstone National Park, Wyoming, Montana, Idaho

Custer State Park, South Dakota

Theodore Roosevelt National Park, North Dakota

National Bison Range, Montana

Henry Mountain, Utah

Wichita Mountains National Wildlife Refuge, Oklahoma

Elk Island, Alberta, Canada

Wood Buffalo National Park, Alberta and Northwest Territories, Canada

Banff National Park, Alberta, Canada

European Bison can be found in Poland: poland.pl/tourism/national-parks/bialowieza
    -national-park/.

EXPLORE

Try your hand at being a conservationist to save condors from extinction. Play Condor
    Country: www.condorcountrygame.com.

Click on the blue dots on the buffalo photo to see how each part of the buffalo was used:
    americanbison.si.edu/american-bison-and-american-indian-nations/.

Explore EDGE species at edgeofexistence.org.

NOTES

THE PATH TO PRESERVATION

"now or never": President Richard Nixon, 51, Special Message to the Congress Outlining the 1972 Environmental Program, Feb. 8, 1972.

"What we really confront here": Richard Nixon: "Statement on Signing the Endangered Species Act of 1973," December 28, 1973. Online by Gerhard Peters and John T. Woolley, The American Presidency Project. www.presidency.ucsb.edu/ws/?pid=4090.

"save a vanishing species": Ibid.

"The purposes of this Act": Endangered Species Act, as amended by P.L. 94-325, June 30, 1976; P.L. 94-359, July 12, 1976; P.L. 95-212, December 19, 1977; P.L. 95-632, November 10, 1978; P.L. 96-159, December 28, 1979; P.L. 97-304, October 13, 1982; P.L. 98-327, June 25, 1984; and P.L. 100-478, October 7, 1988; P.L. 107-171, May 13, 2002; P.L. 108-136, November 24, 2003.

WHOOPING CRANES IN THE WETLANDS

"It was a common thing": William Souder, "How Two Women Ended the Deadly Feather Trade." *Smithsonian,* Mar. 2013: n.p. Accessed Sept. 2016. www.smithsonianmag.com /science-nature/how-two-women-ended-the-deadly-feather-trade-23187277/?page=2.

"We ate lunch": Marjory Stoneman Douglas, The Everglades: River of Grass. New York: Rinehart, 1947, 299.

"For the Whooping crane": Robert P. Allen, *The Whooping Crane,* National Audubon Society Research Report. No. 3, 1952.

WOLVES IN THE WILD

"The wolf is a problem": Bob Bergland, www.eswr.com/docs/lh/426-488.pdf. Endangered Species Act of 1973, Dec. 19, 1973, Report No 93-740, p. 477.

"Life consists with wildness": Henry David Thoreau, "Walking."

"We reached the old wolf": Aldo Leopold, "Thinking Like a Mountain," in *A Sand County Almanac and Sketches Here and There*. New York: Oxford University Press, 1949, Special Commemorative Edition, 1987.

"I now suspect that": Ibid.

"Eventually the wolf took the book": Mowat, *Never Cry Wolf*, preface.

"In the whole of the continental": Ibid.

BALD EAGLES FLY HIGH

"New York has been a leader": Commissioner Basil Seggos, Nov. 30, 2016, email.

"Eagles were the one thing": Pete Nye interview with Paul Grondahl, *Adirondack Explorer*, Feb. 21, 2011.

GIANT GALÁPAGOS TORTOISES WALK THE EARTH

"foolishly tame": www.galapagosislands.com/info/history/.

"The meat of this animal": Beebe, *Galápagos*, 208.

"The people employ": Charles Darwin, *Beagle* diary, September 1835, 362.

"It is only within the last few years": Beebe, *Galápagos*, 213.

"But instead of three custom-house": Herman Melville, The Great Short Works of Herman Melville: The Encantados or Enchanted Isles

CALIFORNIA CONDORS SOAR AGAIN

"Even that day was spooky": David Smollar, "California's Last Condor in Wild Captured," *Los Angeles Times*, April 20, 1987.

"I saw a puff of smoke": Janet Hamber, personal interview with Nancy Castaldo November 18, 2016

"Watching this California condor": "California Condor 'Instrumental in Recovery of Species' Returns to Wild in Kern County," www.nbclosangeles.com/news/local/California-Condor-Returns-Wild-Kern-County-363944051.html.

AMERICAN ALLIGATORS SWIM IN THE SOUTH

"using their faces as shovels": Ted Levin, *Liquid Land: A Journey Through the Florida Everglades.* Athens: University of Georgia Press, 2004, 87.

"The alligator dominated": Frank C. Craighead, 1968. "The role of the alligator in shaping plant communities and maintaining wildlife in the Southern Everglades." *Florida Naturalist,* 41:2–7.

"Three persons residing in the parish": *Lafayette Daily Advertiser,* June 3, 1882.

"The price of the hides": Ibid.

AMERICAN BISON: GIVE ME A HOME WHERE THE BUFFALO ROAM . . .

"darkened the whole plains": Bernard DeVoto, ed., *The Journals of Lewis and Clark.* Boston: Houghton Mifflin, 1953.

"now such an event": William T. Hornaday, quoted in Leslie Allen, "Back Home on the Range," *Smithsonian Magazine,* Feb. 2005 www.smithsonianmag.com/science-nature/back-home-on-the-range-85961623.

"A solitary hunter": Bob Drury and Tom Clavin, *The Heart of Everything That Is: The Untold Story of Red Cloud.* New York: Simon & Schuster, 2013. 183.

"A cold wind blew": Valerius Geist, *Buffalo Nation: History and Legacy of the North American Bison.* Minneapolis: VoyaguerPress, 102.

"There is no reason to hope": Stefan Bechtel, *Mr. Hornaday's War.* Boston: Beacon Press, 2012, 123.

"When people went looking for": Dr. James Derr, personal correspondence.

CALL TO ACTION!

"I believe it's going to be one of the major battles": Russell Peterson, *Palm Beach Post,* Jan. 18, 1982, 9.

BIBLIOGRAPHY

"The Alligator Rescued," *Palm Beach Post,* June 7, 1970.

Allen, Leslie. "Back Home on the Range." *Smithsonian, February 2005.* www.smithson ianmag.com/heritage/back-home-on-the-range-85961623/?no-ist=&page=2.

Barrett, Cindi, and Thomas V. Stehn. "A Retrospective of Whooping Cranes in Captivity." (2010) North American Crane Workshop Proceedings. Paper 110. digitalcommons .unl.edu/nacwgproc/110.

Beebe, William. *Galápagos: World's End.* New York: G. P. Putnam, 1994.

Breining, Greg. "Fifty Shades of Green." *National Wildlife (Oct./Nov. 2015):* 41.

Brown, David, ed. *The Wolf in the Southwest: The Making of an Endangered Species.* Tucson: University of Arizona Press, 1984.

California Condor Habitat Program. National Audubon Society, Western Regional Office, 1984.

California Condor Recovery Program Annual Report, Hopper Mountain National Wildlife Refuge Complex, 2013.

California Condor Recovery Team. *California Condor Recovery Plan.* U.S. Fish and Wildlife Service, 1975.

Caporaso, Fred. "The Galapagos Tortoise Conservation Program: The Plight and Future for the Pinzon Island Tortoise." California Turtle and Tortoise Club, n.d. Accessed Oct. 2, 2015.

Carlton, Jim. "California Island Foxes Recover from Brink of Extinction." *Wall Street*

Journal, August 11, 2016. www.wsj.com/articles/california-island-foxes-recover
-from-brink-of-extinction-1470945601.

Carson, Rachel. *Silent Spring.* Boston: Houghton Mifflin, 1962.

Conservation Plan for Bald Eagles in New York State, New York State Department of
Environmental Conservation, January 2015.

Department of the Interior—Notices—Office of the Secretary, Native Fish and Wildlife
"Endangered Species." *Federal Register,* Vol. 32, No. 48 (March 11, 1967). ecos.fws
.gov/docs/federal_register/fr18.pdf.

Doughty, Robin W. *Return of the Whooping Crane.* Austin: University of Texas Press,
1989.

Drewien, Roderick C. "Teamwork Helps the Whooping Crane." *National Geographic*
(May 1979): 680–92.

"Eagles' Protection in Question: Endangered Species Act May Be Endangered Species."
Lawrence Journal-World, January 24, 1982.

Finkelstein, Myra E., et al. "Lead Poisoning and the Deceptive Recovery of the Criti-
cally Endangered California Condor." *Proceedings of the National Academy of
Sciences of the United States of America* 109.28 (2012): 11449–54. PMC. Accessed
Mar. 17, 2017.

Fortin, Daniel, et al. "Wolves Influence Elk Movements: Behavior Shapes a Trophic
Cascade in Yellowstone National Park." *Ecology* 86.5 (2005): 1320–30.

Geist, Valerius. *Buffalo Nation: History and Legend of the North American Bison.* Minneapolis: Voyageur Press, 1996.

Greenwald, Noah, Amy W. Ando, Stuart H. M. Butchart, and John Tschirhart. "Conservation: The Endangered Species Act at 40." December 18, 2013. www.nature.com
/news?conservation-the-endangered-species-act-at-40-1.14365.

Hampton, Bruce. *The Great American Wolf.* New York: Henry Holt, 1997.

"Idaho's War on Wolves Escalates." Defenders of Wildlife. N.p., Apr. 21, 2014. Accessed Oct. 2, 2015.

"International Recovery Plan for the Whooping Crane," (third revision) 1980–94, 2006. www.fws.gov/southwest/es/Documents/R2ES/. Whooping_Crane_Recovery _Plan_FINAL_21-July-2006.pdf.

Jones, Amanda. "Galapagos at the Crossroads." *Islands* (April 2016): 25–31.

Kaska, Kathleen. *The Man Who Saved the Whooping Crane: The Robert Porter Allen Story.* Gainesville: University Press of Florida, 2012.

Lueck, Dean. "The Extermination and Conservation of the American Bison." *Journal of Legal Studies* 31.S2 (2002): S609–S652

Lynch, Mike. "The Wolf at Our Door." *Adirondack Explorer,* February 23, 2015. www .adirondackexplorer.org/stories/wolf-door.

Main, Douglas. "Galapagos Giant Tortoise Brought Back from Brink of Extinction." *Newsweek,* October 28, 2014. www.newsweek.com/galapagos-giant-tortoise -brought-back-brink-extinction-280593.

Mech, L. David, and Luigi Boitani, eds. *Wolves: Behavior, Ecology, and Conservation.* Chicago: University of Chicago Press, 2010.

Meretsky, Vicky J., et al. "Demography of the California Condor: Implications for Reestablishment." *Conservation Biology* 14.4 (2000): 957–67.

Mowat, Farley. *Never Cry Wolf.* New York: Bantam Books, 1973.

Mueller, Thomas, et al. "Social Learning of Migratory Performance." *Science* 30 (Aug. 2013): 999–1002.

New York's Wintering Bald Eagles. New York State Dept. of Environmental Conservation, March 3, 1983

Nuwer, Rachel. "New Species of Galapagos Tortoise Found on Santa Cruz Island." *Smithsonian,* Oct. 21, 2015. Accessed Mar. 10, 2016.

O'Neil, Roger. "Sioux Are Pleased with 'Dances with Wolves.'" NBC *Today,* Mar. 25, 1991. Accessed January 17, 2016. archives.nbclearn.com/portal/site/k-12/flatview ?cuecard=36359.

Phillips, Michael K., and Douglas W. Smith. *The Wolves of Yellowstone.* Minneapolis: Voyageur Press, 1996.

"Recovery Plan for the U.S. Population of Atlantic Green Turtle." Prepared by the Loggerhead/ Green Turtle Recovery Team for Southeast Region, U.S. Fish and Wildlife Service, 1991.

Radiolab podcast. "Galapagos."

Ripple, William J., and Robert L. Beschta. "Wolves and the Ecology of Fear: Can Predation Risk Structure Ecosystem?" *BioScience* 54.8 (2004): 755–66.

Rudloe, Anne, and Jack Rudloe. "Sea Turtles: In a Race for Survival." *National Geographic,* Vol. 185, No. 2 (February 1994): 94–120.

Snyder, Noel F. R., and Helen Snyder. *The California Condor: A Saga of Natural History and Conservation.* San Diego: Academic Press, 2000.

Steadman, David W., and Steven Zousmer. *Galapagos: Discovery on Darwin's Islands.* Washington, D.C.: Smithsonian Institution Press, 1984.

Watson, Traci. "Rare Butterflies Flying High at Los Angeles Airport." *National Geographic,* April 21, 2016. news.nationalgeographic.com/2016/04/160421-butterflies -endangered-species-animals/.

Wilbur, Sanford R. "The California Condor, 1966–76: A Look at Its Past and Future." No FWS-72. Patuxent Wildlife Research Center, Laurel, Maryland, 1978.

GLOSSARY

alien species—not from outer space, but rather an introduced species of plant or animal that is not native to the area it is in.

biodiversity—the variety of life in the world, or in an ecosystem.

captive breeding—breeding an animal in the controlled environment of a zoo or wildlife reserve.

carapace—the upper shell of a turtle or tortoise.

chelation—a treatment that removes a heavy metal (lead) from the blood intravenously.

commodity—a product that can be bought and sold.

crop—a pouch in a bird's throat where partially digested food is held.

delisted—removal from the Endangered Species List when a species' population has risen to an acceptable number.

endangered—in danger of becoming extinct.

endemic—native to an area.

extirpated—eradicated from an area.

extinction—the process by which an animal or plant species vanishes from the earth.

fledge—to develop flight feathers and leave the nest.

microtrash—tiny pieces of trash, such as bottle caps.

migration—seasonal movement from one place to another.

pesticide—a chemical created to kill pests, usually insects.

predator—an animal that preys on other animals.

reintroduction—the process of introducing a species into an area where it once lived.

sterilize—to surgically make an animal unable to reproduce.

trophic cascade—an ecological occurrence triggered by the addition or removal of a top predator, resulting in dramatic changes in the ecosystem.

ACKNOWLEDGMENTS

There are countless people who work tirelessly on behalf of wildlife. I was privileged to spend time with many of them and want to thank them for sharing their research: Nadya Faith, Andy Bingle, Jan Hamber, Regan Downey, Maggie Howell, James Derr, Jenny Schmidt, Debbie Sears, and George Steele. I greatly admire their work and their perseverance. They are all my heroes.

I want to also thank my kid-lit friends Judy Bryan and Pam Beres, who hosted me on my Wisconsin research trip. They not only spent time with me researching whooping cranes, but together we hiked the paths around Aldo Leopold's shack. (They also fed me cheese curds!)

My endless search for bald eagles in New York would not have been fruitful if it weren't for Jacqueline Rogers and my local Audubon birders! Just as in Jane Yolen's *Owl Moon,* "sometimes there's an owl and sometimes there isn't" was certainly true on those eagle searches!

I also want to thank my writer pals Lois Huey, Anita Sanchez, and my WOW crit group for reading some tough stories about endangered species and listening to my speeches about the importance of the Endangered Species Act.

Jennifer Laughran, agent and friend, helped me find my story. Erica Zappy helped give it a voice! Many thanks to them both and the HMH team for their wonderful support and creativity.

Lastly, my endless gratitude goes out to my husband and daughter for always being willing to go on another adventure with me. They are my joy!

INDEX

Page references in *italics* indicate photographs.